1 JOHN

J. Vernon McGee

THOMAS NELSON PUBLISHERS

Nashville • Atlanta • London • Vancouver

Published in Nashville, Tennessee, by Thomas Nelson, Inc.

Scripture quotations are from the KING JAMES VERSION of the Bible.

Library of Congress Cataloging-in-Publication Data

McGee, J. Vernon (John Vernon), 1904–1988
   [Thru the Bible with J. Vernon McGee]
   Thru the Bible commentary series / J. Vernon McGee.
     p.   cm.
   Reprint. Originally published: Thru the Bible with J. Vernon McGee. 1975.
   Includes bibliographical references.
   ISBN 0-7852-1062-8 (TR)
   ISBN 0-7852-1119-5 (NRM)
   1. Bible—Commentaries. I. Title.
BS491.2.M37 1991
220.7′7—dc20
                       90–41340
                         CIP

PRINTED IN MEXICO
15 16 17 18 19 20 – 10 09 08 07

CONTENTS

1 JOHN

PREFACE

The radio broadcasts of the Thru the Bible Radio five-year program were transcribed, edited, and published first in single-volume paperbacks to accommodate the radio audience.

There has been a minimal amount of further editing for this publication. Therefore, these messages are not the word-for-word recording of the taped messages which went out over the air. The changes were necessary to accommodate a reading audience rather than a listening audience.

These are popular messages, prepared originally for a radio audience. They should not be considered a commentary on the entire Bible in any sense of that term. These messages are devoid of any attempt to present a theological or technical commentary on the Bible. Behind these messages is a great deal of research and study in order to interpret the Bible from a popular rather than from a scholarly (and too-often boring) viewpoint.

We have definitely and deliberately attempted "to put the cookies on the bottom shelf so that the kiddies could get them."

The fact that these messages have been translated into many languages for radio broadcasting and have been received with enthusiasm reveals the need for a simple teaching of the whole Bible for the masses of the world.

I am indebted to many people and to many sources for bringing this volume into existence. I should express my especial thanks to my secretary, Gertrude Cutler, who supervised the editorial work; to Dr. Elliott R. Cole, my associate, who handled all the detailed work with the publishers; and finally, to my wife Ruth for tenaciously encouraging me from the beginning to put my notes and messages into printed form.

Solomon wrote, ". . . of making many books there is no end; and much study is a weariness of the flesh" (Eccl. 12:12). On a sea of books that flood the marketplace, we launch this series of THRU THE BIBLE with the hope that it might draw many to the one Book, *The Bible.*

J. VERNON McGEE

1 JOHN

The First Epistle of

JOHN

INTRODUCTION

Some expositors consider the epistles of John to be the final books written in the Bible. Certainly John's epistles are the last which he wrote.

The three epistles are called letters; yet the first epistle is not in the form or style of a letter. It has no salutation at its beginning nor greeting at its conclusion. Its style is more that of a sermon. It bears all the marks of a message from a devoted pastor who had a love and concern for a definite group of believers.

John served as pastor of the church in Ephesus, which was founded by Paul. It has been the belief of the church down through the years that John wrote his Gospel first, his epistles second, and finally the Revelation just before his death. However, in recent years some of us have come to the position that John wrote his epistles last. Therefore, he wrote his first epistle after his imprisonment on the Island of Patmos. This places the date about A.D. 100. John died in Ephesus and was buried there. The Basilica of St. John was built over the grave of John by Justinian in the fifth century.

To understand the First Epistle of John we must know something about the city of Ephesus at the beginning of the second century. It was very much like your city or hometown today. There were four important factors which prevailed in Ephesus and throughout the Roman world:

1. There was an easy familiarity with Christianity. Many of the believers were children and grandchildren of the first Christians. The new and bright sheen of the Christian faith had become tarnished.

The newness had worn off. The thrill and glory of the first days had faded. My, how exciting it had been to be a believer on that day when Paul had come to town and challenged Diana of the Ephesians! The whole town had been in an uproar. In Acts 19 we read of the effect Paul's teaching had upon the synagogue at Ephesus and also the impact of his daily sessions in the school of Tyrannus for two years. How fervent their love and zeal for Christ had been in those days. But many years later, when the Lord Jesus sent a letter to the Ephesian believers through John while he was in exile on the Island of Patmos, He said, "Nevertheless I have somewhat against thee, because thou hast left thy first love" (Rev. 2:4). It was as Jesus had long before warned, ". . . because iniquity shall abound, the love of many shall wax cold" (Matt. 24:12). The Ephesians' devotion and dedication to Christ was at a low ebb.

2. The high standards of Christianity made the Christians different, and the children and grandchildren of the first Christians did not want to be different. The believers were called saints—from the Greek word *hagios*. The primary intent of the word is "set aside for the sole use of God—that which belongs to God." The pots and pans in the temple were said to be holy because they were for the use of God. The temple was *hagios*; the Sabbath was *hagios*. Now the Christians were to be *hagios*—different, set aside for the use of God.

But the Ephesians had become assembly-line Christians, programmed by the computer of compromise. They had become plastic Christians. They were cast in a different mold from the disciples to whom Jesus had said, "If ye were of the world, the world would love his own: but because ye are not of the world, but I have chosen you out of the world, therefore the world hateth you" (John 15:19). And also in His high priestly prayer to His Father are these words: "I have given them thy word; and the world hath hated them, because they are not of the world, even as I am not of the world" (John 17:14). There was a breakdown of the Judeo-Christian ethic and a disregard of Bible standards.

3. Persecution was not the enemy of Christianity. The danger to the Ephesian church was not persecution from the outside but seduction from the inside. The Lord Jesus Himself had warned of this: "For

there shall arise false Christs, and false prophets, and shall shew great signs and wonders; insomuch that, if it were possible, they shall deceive the very elect" (Matt. 24:24). And the apostle Paul had said to the Ephesian elders: "For I know this, that after my departing shall grievous wolves enter in among you, not sparing the flock. Also of your own selves shall men arise, speaking perverse things, to draw away disciples after them" (Acts 20:29–30).

Christianity was not in danger of being destroyed; it was in danger of being changed. The attempt was being made to improve it, give it intellectual respectability, and let it speak in the terms of the popular philosophy.

4. Gnosticism was the real enemy of Christianity, and, my friend, it still is. Gnosticism was the basic philosophy of the Roman Empire.

Gnosticism took many forms. However, one primary principle ran through this philosophy: matter of material was essentially evil; only the spirit was good. All the material world was considered evil. Therefore Gnosticism despised the body. They held that in the body was a spirit, like a seed in the dirty soil. The same principle is in modern liberalism which maintains that there is a spark of good in everyone and that each person is to develop that spark of good. The Gnostics sought to cause the "seed," the spirit within them, to grow and tried to get rid of the evil in the body.

There were two extreme methods of accomplishing this goal as practiced by the Stoics and the Epicureans. The apostle Paul's encounter with these two sects is recorded in Acts 17:18: "Then certain philosophers of the Epicureans, and of the Stoics, encountered him. And some said, What will this babbler say? other some, He seemeth to be a setter forth of strange gods: because he preached unto them Jesus and the resurrection."

The Stoics were disciples of Zeno, and their name came from the Painted Portico at Athens where Zeno lectured. They were pantheists who held that the wise men should be free from passion, unmoved by joy or grief, and submissive to natural law. They observed rigid rules and self-discipline.

The Epicureans took their name from Epicurus who taught in Athens. They accepted the Greek gods on Mount Olympus. They considered pleasure rather than truth the pursuit of life. Originally they sought to satisfy intellectual, not sensual, gratification; but later they taught their followers to satisfy the body's desires so it wouldn't bother them any more.

There were all shades and differences between the two extremes of Stoicism and Epicureanism, but all of them denied the messiahship of Jesus. I believe John had them in mind when he wrote: "Who is a liar but he that denieth that Jesus is the Christ? He is antichrist, that denieth the Father and the Son" (1 John 2:22). They denied the Incarnation, reasoning that God could not have taken a human body because all flesh is evil. Therefore John distinctly declared, "And the Word was made [born] flesh, and dwelt among us, (and we beheld his glory, the glory as of the only begotten of the Father,) full of grace and truth" (John 1:14). And in his epistle he wrote: "Hereby know ye the Spirit of God: Every spirit that confesseth that Jesus Christ is come in the flesh is of God: And every spirit that confesseth not that Jesus Christ is come in the flesh is not of God: and this is that spirit of antichrist, whereof ye have heard that it should come; and even now already is it in the world" (1 John 4:2-3).

Docetic Gnosticism, considering the Incarnation impossible since God could not unite Himself with anything evil such as a body, taught that Jesus only *seemed* to have a body, but actually He did not. For example, when He walked He left no footprints.

Cerinthus was more subtle in his teaching. He declared that there was both a human Jesus and a divine Christ, that divinity came upon Him at His baptism and left Him at the Cross. In fact, the Gospel of Peter, which is a spurious book, translates the words of Jesus on the Cross like this: "My power, my power, why hast thou forsaken me?"

The early church fathers fought this heresy and maintained that "He became what we are to make us what He is." It is my firm opinion that John wrote his first epistle to answer the errors of Gnosticism. Actually there is a fivefold purpose expressed in 1 John: (1) 1:3, "That ye also may have fellowship with us [other believers]: and . . . with the Father, and with his Son Jesus Christ;" (2) 1:4, "That your joy may be full;" (3) 2:1, "That ye sin not;" (4) 5:13, "That ye may know that ye have eternal life;" and (5) 5:13, "That ye may believe on the name of the Son of God."

First John has been called the *sanctum sanctorum* of the New Testament. It takes the child of God across the threshold into the fellowship of the Father's home. It is the *family* epistle. Paul's epistles and all the other epistles are church epistles, but this is a family epistle and should be treated that way. The church is a body of believers in the position where we are blessed ". . . with all spiritual blessings in the heavenlies in Christ" (Eph. 1:3, translation mine). We are given that position when we believe on the Lord Jesus Christ. Believing on the Lord Jesus brings us into the family of God. In the family we have a relationship which can be broken but is restored when "we confess our sins." Then "he is faithful and just to forgive us our sins, and to cleanse us from all unrighteousness" (1 John 1:9).

First John is the book which I used when I began my ministry in a new church. (I didn't at the first church I served because I was a seminary student and didn't know enough to begin in the right place.) But in the four churches I served during my forty years of pastoring, I began the midweek service with a study in 1 John. I am convinced that this epistle is more important for believers in the church than the church epistles. When we moved into this wonderful book, I saw the midweek service attendance increase. We saw a phenomenal increase in attendance in the last two churches I served. During the time we studied this little epistle the attendance doubled, doubled again, and then doubled again, so that we had as many people in attendance at the midweek service as we had in the Sunday evening service. Sometimes the midweek service would surpass the Sunday night service. My friend, it is *very* important to understand this little book.

OUTLINE

In 1 John there are three definitions of God: God is *light*, God is *love*, and God is *life*, which I have used to form the three major divisions of this epistle.

I. God Is Light (1:5), Chapters 1:1—2:2
  A. Prologue, Chapter 1:1-2
  B. How the Little Children May Have Fellowship with God, Chapters 1:3—2:2
    1. By Walking in Light, Chapter 1:3-7
    2. By Confessing Sin, Chapter 1:8-10
    3. By the Advocacy of Christ, Chapter 2:1-2

II. God Is Love (4:8), Chapters 2:3—4:21
  A. How the Dear Children May Have Fellowship with Each Other, Chapter 2:3-14
     (*By Walking in Love*)
  B. The Dear Children Must Not Love the World, Chapter 2:15-28
  C. How the Dear Children May Know Each Other and Live Together, Chapters 2:29—4:21
    1. The Father's Love for His Children, Chapters 2:29—3:3
    2. The Two Natures of the Believer in Action, Chapter 3:4-24
    3. Warning Against False Teachers, Chapter 4:1-6
    4. God Is Love: Little Children Will Love Each Other, Chapter 4:7-21

III. God Is Life (5:12), Chapter 5
  A. Victory Over the World, Chapter 5:1-5
  B. Assurance of Salvation, Chapter 5:6-21

CHAPTER 1

THEME: God is light; how the little children may have fellowship with God

Under the broad heading, God is Light, we see first the prologue of this epistle, then we shall see how the "little children," as John calls believers, may have fellowship with God.

As I mentioned in the Introduction, John has written to meet the first heresy which entered the church, Gnosticism. The Gnostics boasted of a superknowledge. They accepted the deity of Jesus but denied His humanity. Notice how John will give the true gnosticism—that is, the true knowledge of God.

GOD IS LIGHT: PROLOGUE

That which was from the beginning, which we have heard, which we have seen with our eyes, which we have looked upon, and our hands have handled, of the Word of life [1 John 1:1].

"That which was from the beginning." What beginning is John talking about? In the Scriptures are three beginnings, two of which we are very familiar with. The first is found in Genesis 1:1: "In the beginning God created the heaven and the earth." That is an undated beginning. We do not know *when* God created the heaven and the earth. I have read book after book, volume after volume, on the questions raised by the first chapter of Genesis. If I stacked up all those books, I am confident that they would reach the ceiling of my study. And after reading all of them, I am convinced that not one scientist or one theologian has the foggiest notion when Genesis 1:1 really happened.

I am told that today there are some Christian scientists who are taking what they call the "new earth view." They are claiming that the earth on which we live is not as old as the science of the past claimed it to be.

When I started school it was estimated that the earth was three to seven hundred thousand years old. Then science began to speak in terms of millions of years. By the time I finished school it was estimated that the earth was about 2½ million years old, and then, I understand, they reached the billion mark.

Now some scientists are moving away from the older dating of the earth and are setting a more recent date. Well, Genesis 1:1 would fit into either theory, a new earth or an old earth, since it is not dated. All that the first verse in Genesis declares is that God created the heaven and the earth. Until you are ready to accept that fact, you are not prepared to read very much further in the Word of God, because the remainder of the Bible rests upon that first verse. Did God create this universe or is it a happenstance? It is ridiculous to think that the universe just happened. As Edwin Conklin put it, "The probability of life originating by accident is comparable to the probability of the unabridged dictionary originating from an explosion in a print shop." My friend, there is intelligence behind this universe in which you and I live. As to the date of the beginning, we do not know; but if you need a few billion years to fit into your scheme of interpretation, it is here because we are dealing with the God of eternity. God has eternity behind Him. Although I don't know what He was doing before He created the heaven and the earth, I know He was doing something. Then God created the heaven and the earth, and He did it for a purpose. He is working out a plan in His universe today which is bigger than any human mind can comprehend. When God recorded His act of creation, He wasn't trying to give us a study in geology. However, He put a lot of rocks around for you to look at if you are interested in trying to figure out a date.

There is a second beginning which we find in the Word of God. It is the first verse in John's Gospel: "In the beginning was the Word, and the Word was with God, and the Word was God." He adds, "The same was in the beginning with God." Then he comes to the act of creation: "All things were made by him; and without him was not any thing made that was made" (John 1:1–3). My friend, go back as far as you can think, beyond creation, back billions and trillions of years, and out of eternity comes the Lord Jesus Christ. Way back there He is already past tense; He is the Ancient of Days. Notice that John has written, "In the beginning *was* [not *is*] the Word." In other words, this is a beginning that doesn't even have a beginning because He had no beginning. "In the beginning *was* the Word" means that you can go back in the past as far as you want to, put down your peg anywhere, and Christ comes out of eternity to meet you. That is big stuff; it is bigger than my little mind can comprehend. I am unable to grasp the immensity of it until I come to John 1:14: "And the Word was made [born] flesh. . . ." That takes me back to Bethlehem where He was born, and I begin to catch on at that time.

The third beginning is the one we began with in 1 John 1:1—"That which was from the beginning," which refers to the time Christ came into this world at Bethlehem. When He was about thirty years old, John became acquainted with Him. John and his brother James met Him in Jerusalem. Later they were with their father, mending nets, when Jesus came by and called them to follow Him. They left their father (probably a well-to-do fisherman) with the hired men and followed Jesus. Now John says, I want to tell you about Him, and he asserts the reality of the total personality of Jesus: (1) "We have heard" (through the ear-gate); (2) "we have seen" (through the eye-gate); (3) "we have looked upon" (lit., *gazed intently* upon); and (4) "our hands have handled."

John, of course, is speaking of the incarnation of Jesus and of his own association with Him when He was here upon this earth.

"Which we have heard." John is not prattling about his opinions and his speculations. He is talking about the fact that he *heard* the Lord Jesus, heard His voice, and when he listened to Him, he listened to God.

"Which we have seen with our eyes." Not only had the apostles heard Him speak, but they also had seen Him with their own eyes. In our day we cannot see Him with our physical eyes, but we can see Him with the eye of faith. Peter told us, "Whom having not seen, ye love; in whom, though now ye see him not, yet believing, ye rejoice with joy unspeakable and full of glory" (1 Pet. 1:8). And the Lord Jesus said to Thomas, who would not believe He had been resurrected until he could see and handle Him, ". . . Thomas, because thou hast seen me, thou hast believed: blessed are they that have not seen, and yet have believed" (John 20:29). We today are walking by faith, and the Lord Jesus Christ can be made as real to us as He was to Thomas. As the hymn writer expressed it—

> But warm, sweet, tender, even yet
> A present help is He;
> And faith has still its Olivet,
> And love its Galilee.
>
> "We May Not Climb"
> —John G. Whittier

"Which we have looked upon." The word *looked* is from the Greek word *theaomai* from which we get our English word *theatre*, meaning "to gaze intently upon." The theatre is a place where you sit and look, not just with a passing glance but with a gaze—a steady gaze for a couple of hours. John is saying that for three years they gazed upon Jesus. It was John who wrote, "And as Moses lifted up the serpent in the wilderness, even so must the Son of man be lifted up" (John 3:14). During the wilderness march, the people who had been bitten by the serpents were to look for healing to that brass serpent which had been lifted up on a pole. John is applying that to the Lord Jesus and saying that now we are to look to Him in faith for salvation. After we have done that, we are to gaze upon Him—and we will do that in this epistle. To look, saves; to gaze, sanctifies. John wrote in his Gospel, "And the Word was made flesh, and dwelt among us, (and we beheld his glory, the glory as of the only begotten of the Father,) full of grace and truth" (John 1:14). Many of us need to do more than simply look to Him for salvation. We need to spend time gazing upon Him with the eye of faith.

"Our hands have handled." John says that they did more than merely gaze upon Him from a distance; they handled Him. John himself reclined upon His bosom in the Upper Room. Speaking to His own after His resurrection, He said, "Behold my hands and my feet, that it is I myself: handle me, and see; for a spirit hath not flesh and bones, as ye see me have. And when he had thus spoken, he shewed them his hands and his feet" (Luke 24:39–40).

Dr. G. Campbell Morgan takes the position that when the Lord Jesus held out His hands to Thomas and to the other disciples, they were so overwhelmed that they did not handle Him. Instead, they bowed down in reverence to Him. That would be the normal thing to do, but John makes it clear that they handled the Lord. This is one place where I disagree with Dr. Morgan, (and I disagree with him in a few other places, too) but I dare not disagree with a man of his caliber unless there is a reason for it. But when John says that they handled Him, I think he means they *felt* His hands and fingered the nailprints which convinced them that He was indeed man, the Word made flesh, God manifest in the flesh.

After the death of Paul, about A.D. 67, a heresy arose in the church called Gnosticism. Gnosticism is the opposite of agnosticism. Agnosticism holds that the reality of God is unknown and probably unknowable. There are many agnostics in our colleges and universities, as you know. Charles Spurgeon used to say that *agnostic* is but the Greek word for the Latin *ignoramus*. So one might say, "I don't believe the Bible, because I am an ignoramus!" The agnostic says, "I do not know." The Gnostic says, "I *do* know." The Gnostics were a group which came into the church claiming to have a superior knowledge which simple Christians did not have. They considered themselves super-duper saints, knowing more than anyone else knew.

The Gnostics came up with quite a few novel ideas, which I have dealt with in more detail in the Introduction. One of their heretical teachings was that Jesus was merely a man when He was born. He was just like any other human being at the time of His birth, but at His baptism, the Christ came upon him, and when He was hanging on the Cross, the Christ left Him. John refutes this teaching in no uncertain terms when he said in his Gospel record, "The Word was *born* flesh." And here in his first epistle, he emphatically declares that after Jesus came back from the dead, He was still a human being. In essence John says, "We *handled* Him—He was still flesh and bones." You see, John is not talking about a theory. He is talking about Someone he heard, he saw, and he handled.

> (For the life was manifested, and we have seen it, and
> bear witness, and shew unto you that eternal life, which
> was with the Father, and was manifested unto us;)
> [1 John 1:2].

"For the life was manifested." That is, the life was brought out into the open where men could see it. John is talking about the Word of Life, the Lord Jesus Christ, as we shall see in the next verse.

On one occasion after I had given a message, a man whom I would call a smart aleck came to me with this question: "You talked about eternal life. What is eternal life? I would like to know what eternal life is." So I gave him this verse: "The life was manifested, and we have seen it, and bear witness, and shew unto you that eternal life, which was with the Father, and was manifested unto us." Then I said to him, "The eternal life that John is talking about is none other than Jesus Christ. If you want a definition, eternal life is a Person, and that Person is Christ. It is so simple that even you can grasp it. You either have Christ, or you don't have Christ. You either trust Christ, or you don't trust Christ. If you do trust Christ, you have *eternal life*. If you don't trust Christ, you don't have eternal life. Now since that's eternal life, do *you* have eternal life?" He turned and walked away without answering, which was an evidence that he did not have eternal life, and he did not want to pursue the matter any further.

HOW TO HAVE FELLOWSHIP WITH GOD

Now John is going to say something which is quite wonderful. He is going to tell us that we can have fellowship with God! One of the most glorious prospects before us today is that you and I can have fellowship with God.

> That which we have seen and heard declare we unto
> you, that ye also may have fellowship with us: and truly
> our fellowship is with the Father, and with his Son Jesus
> Christ [1 John 1:3].

"That which we have seen and heard"—this is the third time he has said this, and it should be penetrating our consciousnesses by now.

Why, John, are you repeating this? "That ye also may have fellowship with us." He is saying that believers can have fellowship one with another.

"And truly our fellowship is with the Father, and with his Son Jesus Christ." How are we ever going to have fellowship with God? It does present a dilemma. God is holy. Man is unholy. How can this gulf be bridged? How can you bring God and man together, or as Amos put it, "Can two walk together, except they be agreed?" (Amos 3:3). How are we going to have fellowship? To get over this seemingly impossible hurdle, John is going to present three methods. Two of them are man-made methods and won't work. The other one is God's method, and it is the only one that will work.

Before we get into that, let me say a word about the word *fellowship*. *Fellowship* is the Greek word *koinōnia*, and it means "having in common or sharing with." Christian fellowship means sharing the things of Christ. And to do this, we must know the Lord Jesus—not only know about Him, but know Him as our personal Savior.

In our day we have lost the true meaning of the word *fellowship*. Let me give you an example of what I mean. Several years ago I used to go to Huntington Beach in Southern California and speak to a Rotary Club. A wonderful doctor who was the program chairman told me that they could probably take me once a year; so he invited me for either Christmas or Easter and told me to give them both barrels. (I tried to give them both barrels, and since he is no longer program chairman, they haven't invited me back!) One of the things I noticed in the place where the Rotary Club met was a large banner over the elevated speaker's table with the words, "Fun, Food, Fellowship." Well, the food was nothing to brag about—embalmed chicken and peas as big as bullets. The fun was corny jokes. The fellowship consisted of one man patting another on the back and saying, "Hi, Bill, how's business?" or, "How's the wife?" Then they sang a little song together. That was their idea of fellowship.

Well, the Christian idea of fellowship is not much different. When you hear an announcement of a church banquet, it is almost certain that you will be urged to come for food and fellowship. What do they mean by fellowship? They mean meeting around the table and talking to each other about everything under the sun except the one thing that would give them true fellowship, the person of Christ.

Now let me give you an illustration of one place where the word *fellowship* is used correctly. I had the privilege of being at Oxford University as a tourist and seeing the Great Quad, the Wren Tower, and the different schools that comprise Oxford University. I visited one school which specialized in Shakespeare. Now suppose you wanted to know all about Shakespeare because you wanted to teach that particular subject. You would go to Oxford University and attend the particular school specializing in that subject. When you ate, you would sit down at the board, and there you would meet the other men who were studying Shakespeare, and you would meet the professors who did the teaching. You would hear them all talking about Shakespeare in a way you never had heard before. For instance, in the play *Romeo and Juliet* most of us think that Juliet was the only girl Romeo courted. It is shocking to find that when he said,

"One fairer than my love! the all-seeing sun
Ne'er saw her match since first the world begun,"

that fickle fellow Romeo was talking about another girl! You would hear many things that would alert you to the fact that you had a lot to learn about Shakespeare. So you would begin to study and pull books off the shelf in the library and go to the lectures. After you had been at the school for two or three years, they would make you a fellow. Then when you would go in and sit at the board with the other students and professors, you would join right in with them as they talked about the sonnets of Shakespeare. You would have *fellowship* with them, sharing the things of Shakespeare.

Now fellowship for the believer means that we meet and share the things of Christ. We talk together about the Lord Jesus Christ and His Word. That is the kind of fellowship that John is speaking of when he says, "That ye also may have fellowship with us: and truly our fellow-ship is with the Father, and with his Son Jesus Christ."

WALK IN LIGHT

And these things write we unto you, that your joy may be full [1 John 1:4].

Now this is the second reason he mentions for writing his epistle: "That your joy may be full." How wonderful to have joy—not just a little joy but a whole lot of joy because we are experiencing fellow-ship. *Koinōnia* sometimes refers to the *act* of fellowship—the commu-nion service in a church is an *act* of fellowship: giving is an *act* of fellowship, and praying is an *act* of fellowship. But in this chapter John is talking about the *experience* of fellowship, such as Paul had in mind when he wrote, "That I may know him, and the power of his resurrection, and the fellowship of his sufferings . . ." (Phil. 3:10).

My friend, the ultimate aim in preaching is that, through convic-tion and repentance, men and women might come to salvation and that it might bring great joy to their hearts, like the Ethiopian eunuch who came to know Christ with the help of Philip. He didn't continue his trip bragging about what a great preacher Philip was; he went on his way rejoicing. Why? Because he had come to know Christ. The purpose of John's epistle is that you and I might share together these wonderful things of Christ, that the Spirit of God might make the Lord Jesus and the Father real to us in such a way that our fellowship might be sweet.

Now we return to the problem which I mentioned earlier. John has said that he has written these things so that we can have fellowship and so that our joy might be full, and our joy would naturally be full if we could have fellowship with God. However, there is a hurdle to get over. John faces up to a real dilemma which every child of God recog-nizes. The very possibility of man having fellowship with God is one of the most glorious prospects that comes to us, but immediately our hopes are dashed when we face up to this dilemma:

This then is the message which we have heard of him, and declare unto you, that God is light, and in him is no darkness at all [1 John 1:5].

"God is light, and in him is no darkness at all" means that God is holy, and we know that man is unholy. How can the gulf be bridged between a wonderful Savior and Vernon McGee? What a difference there is! The canyon between us is steep and deep. How can God and man be brought together? The cry of Job was for a "daysman" who might lay his hand upon Job and upon God and bring them together (see Job 9:33). Through Isaiah God says, "For my thoughts are not your thoughts, neither are your ways my ways . . ." (Isa. 55:8). How is a sinful man going to walk with God?

John tells us that God is light. This is, in fact, a definition of God. I have divided this epistle into three parts and each part is a definition of God: (1) God is light; (2) God is love; and (3) God is life. But how in the world are we going to have fellowship with God? It looks as if we are going to have to do one of two things. We either have to bring God down to our level, or we will have to take man up to God's level. Neither one of these things can be done, and yet men have tried it. John shows the impossibility of the first one and then gives us a great definition of God: *God is light.*

Modern science, I am told, is not quite sure what light is. Is it energy or is it matter? What is light? Oh, the source of light is one thing, but when you turn on the light in your room, the darkness lurking in the corner becomes light. What has happened? What was it that went over there in the corner and drove out the darkness? Or *did* it drive out the darkness? Because when the source of light up in the ceiling goes off, darkness returns to the corner. What is light?

Well, when John says that God is light, he is revealing many facets about the person of God. Although it doesn't cover the whole spectrum of the attributes of God, it says a great deal about Him.

First of all, light speaks of the glory, the radiance, the beauty, and the wonders of God. Have you seen the eastern sky when the sun comes up like a blaze of glory? A friend and I once camped on the edge of Monument Valley in Arizona. It was a beautiful spot. We spent the night in sleeping bags. When I awoke the next morning, my friend was standing there, watching as the dawn was breaking. I asked him what he was doing up so early, and he made this statement: "I am watching God create a new day." Oh, what a thrill it was to be there and watch God create a new day! All of a sudden the sun peeped over the horizon, then it came marching over in a blaze of glory. I must confess that it became pretty hot later in the day, but what a sunrise it was! God is light. Oh, the beauty and radiance and glory of God!

Another characteristic of light is that it is self-revealing. Light can be seen, but it diffuses itself. It illuminates the darkness. It is revealing. It lets me see my hands—I've been handling books, and I see that one of my hands has dirt on it, and I'm going to have to take it out and wash it. If it hadn't been for the light, I would not have seen the soil. Light reveals flaws and impurity. Whittier put it like this:

> Our thoughts lie open to Thy sight;
> And naked to Thy glance;
> Our secret sins are in the light
> Of Thy pure countenance.

And Dr. Chafer used to say it this way: "Secret sin down here is open scandal in heaven." Our sins are right there before Him, because God is light.

Also light speaks of the white purity of God and the stainless holiness of God. God moves without making a shadow because He is light. He is pure. The light of the sun is actually the cartharsis of the earth. It not only gives light, it is also a great cleanser. Many of you ladies put a garment out in the sun to clean it or to get an odor out of it. The sun is a great cleansing agent. Light speaks of the purity of God.

Light also guides men. It points out the path. Light on the horizon leads men on to take courage. It gives them courage to keep moving on. God is light. Let me go to the other extreme. Darkness is actually more than a negation of light. It is not just the opposite of light. It is actually hostile to light. The light and holiness of God are in direct conflict with the evil darkness and chaos of the world.

Now we are presented with this dilemma. I am a little creature down here on earth, filled with sin. If you want to know the truth, I am totally depraved. Without the grace of God for salvation, I would be nothing in the world but a creature in rebellion against God, with no good within me at all. God has made it very clear that He finds no good within man. Paul says, "For I know that in me (that is, in my flesh,) dwelleth no good thing . . ." (Rom. 7:18). Paul also says, ". . . There is none righteous, no, not one" (Rom. 3:10). Not only have they no innate goodness, but they are in *rebellion* against God.

Paul goes on to tell us about the rebellion that is in the human heart. He says, ". . . the carnal mind is enmity against God: for it is not subject to the law of God, neither indeed can be" (Rom. 8:7). We are living in a world today that is in rebellion against almighty God. God is holy. I am a sinner. I am saved by grace, yes, but how am I going to have fellowship with Him? How am I going to walk with Him? Men have attempted to do this in three different ways which are presented here, and two of those ways are wrong.

REDUCE GOD TO MAN'S LEVEL?

The first method is to bring God down to the level of man.

If we say that we have fellowship with him, and walk in darkness, we lie, and do not the truth [1 John 1:6].

"If we say that we have fellowship with him"—there are a lot of folk claiming to have fellowship with Him when they do not in reality at all.

"We lie, and do not the truth." Do you understand what John says in this verse? He is rather blunt, don't you think so? He says that we lie. It is not a nice thing to call another man a liar. John says that if you say that you have fellowship with God and you walk in darkness— that is, in sin—you are *lying*. I didn't say that. I am too polite to say that, but John said it. We always think of John as being that little lady-like apostle who carried a handkerchief in his sleeve. I don't know how the rumor got started that John was that kind of a man, unless it began during the Middle Ages when an artist painted him with *curls!*

I suppose the artist got the idea of curls from the fact that John is called the apostle of *love*. But our Lord never called him that—He called him a son of thunder! If John and that artist meet on the corner of Glory Avenue and Hallelujah Boulevard in heaven, I tell you, that artist is going to know what thunder and lightning both are, because I think John is going to level with him, "What is the big idea of giving the world the impression that I was a sissy-type individual!" John was a great, big, two-fisted, rugged fisherman, and he is the one who says, "If you say you are having fellowship with God, and you walk in darkness, you *lie*, because God is light; God is holy."

We hear so much about sin among Christians today. One of the headlines in a newspaper here in Southern California told of some members of a cult committing adultery. (I don't know if that report was accurate or not, but I don't think the paper would have risked a lawsuit by printing it if it had no basis of truth.) Yet this cult brags about keeping the Mosaic Law and having reached a wonderful level of life. Of course, one of the Ten Commandments is "Thou shalt not commit adultery" (Exod. 20:14), but they would attempt to explain that away in some manner. My friend, if you are going to walk with God, you are going to walk in *light*. And if there is sin in your life, you are *not* walking with Him. You cannot bring Him down to your level.

But if we walk in the light, as he is in the light, we have fellowship one with another, and the blood of Jesus Christ his Son cleanseth us from all sin [1 John 1:7].

"If we walk in the light," that is, if we walk in the light of the Word of God. Dr. Harry Ironside tells of his own confusion of mind relative to this verse. Noticing that the cleansing of the blood depends upon our walking in the light, he read it as though it said, "If we walk *according to* the light, the blood of Jesus Christ His Son cleanseth us from all sin." He thought it meant that if he was very punctilious about obeying every command of God, God would cleanse him. Then he noticed that it does not say if we walk *according to* light, but if we walk *in* the light. The important thing is *where* we walk, not *how* we walk. Have we come into the presence of God and allowed the Word of God to shine upon our sinful hearts? You see, it is possible to walk in darkness, thinking you are all right.

Let me illustrate this. I went squirrel hunting several years ago when I was holding meetings in my first pastorate in Middle Tennessee in a place called Woodbury. After the morning service a doctor came to me and asked me if I would like to go squirrel hunting, and I told him there was nothing I would rather do. After lunch he brought me a shotgun, and we drove out to his farm and parked in the barnyard. We walked along by the creek there and had some good hunting. FInally we came to a fork in the creek, and he said to me, "I'll take the right fork, and you take the left fork. It will lead you around the hill and back to the barnyard. We will meet there." In the meantime it looked like it was going to rain. It had drizzled once or twice and stopped. When I started out by myself, it started drizzling again. I kept going, and I made the turn around the hill. I noticed quite a few caves in the hill, and when it started to really rain, I knew I was going to get wet; so I crawled into one of those caves. I went into the largest one I could find and sat in that dark cave for about thirty minutes. I began to get cold and decided I needed a fire; so I gathered together a bunch of leaves scattered on the floor of the cave and put a match to them. I soon had a small fire going, and when I looked around the cave, I found out that I wasn't alone. I have never been in a place in which there were so many spiders and lizards as there were in that cave! Over in one corner was a little snake all coiled up, just looking at me. My friend, I got out of there in a hurry, working on the assumption that possession is nine-tenths of the law, and since those creatures had the cave ahead of me, it belonged to them. I proceeded down to the barn and really got soaking wet, but I wasn't going to stay in that cave!

Now let me make an application. I had been sitting in comfort for about thirty minutes while I was in darkness, but when the light of the fire revealed what was in the cave, I could no longer be comfortable there. My friend, across this land today are multitudes of folk who are sitting in churches every Sunday morning but are not hearing the Word of God. As a result, they are sitting there in darkness, hearing some dissertation on economics or politics or the "good life" or an exhortation on doing the best they can. And they are comfortable. Of course, they are comfortable! But if they would get into the light of the Word of God, they would see that they are *sinners* and that they cannot bring God down to their level. John has said that if a person says he is having fellowship with God but is living in sin, he is *lying*.

During my many years as a pastor I have encountered a great deal of this. I think of a layman who was a good speaker and went about giving his testimony to different groups. Then it was discovered that he was living in adultery—for several years he had been keeping a woman on the side. When it was discovered, my, the damage it did to the cause of Christ. And that man still insists that he is having fellowship with God! I recognize that we are living in a day when moral standards are changing drastically and folk rationalize their sinning and try to explain it away, but they *cannot* bring God down to their level. If you are living in sin, God will not have fellowship with you. If you think otherwise, you are fooling yourself or using a psychological ploy to put up a good front. And many of our psychological hang-ups today center around this very point. As someone commented, after hearing me speak on this subject, "What you mean, Dr. McGee, is that there are hypocrites in the church." And when you come right down to the nitty-gritty, that's what we are talking about. Hypocrites. They profess one thing, "I'm having fellowship with God," and all the while they are walking in darkness. John says they are lying.

Now, suppose you are a child of God, and you are living in sin—but you see it now in the light of the Word of God. Have you lost your salvation? When the light in my study revealed that spot of dirt on my hand, I went and washed it off. And John says, "And the blood of Jesus Christ his Son cleanseth us from all sin." That word *cleanseth* is in the present tense—Christ's blood just keeps on cleansing us from all sin. You haven't lost your salvation, but you have lost your fellowship with God until you are cleansed.

You see, John is talking about *family* truth. At the time I am writing this, there is abroad a great emphasis on what is known as *body* truth. Some folk have stumbled onto it for the first time and have gone off the deep end in their overemphasis of it. *Body* truth is great and it is an important part of New Testament teaching, but *family* truth is also important. If you are in the family of God and have sin in your life, God is not going to treat you like the sinner outside of Christ. He is going to treat you like a disobedient child. He will take you to the woodshed for punishment. Remember that He took David to the woodshed, and certainly Ananias and Sapphira didn't get off easily. My friend, our attempt to bring God down to our level simply will not work. However, that is one method which is often used in an attempt to bridge the gap between a holy God and sinful man.

CONFESS SIN

Another method which is often used is an attempt to bring man up to God's level. They say that man has reached sinless perfection and that he is living on that very high plateau. Well, John deals with that approach. Listen to him—

If we say that we have no sin, we deceive ourselves, and the truth is not in us [1 John 1:8].

This is even worse than being a liar. When you get to the place where you say you have no sin in your life, there is no truth in you at all. This doesn't mean you are simply a liar; it means you don't even have the truth. You are deceiving yourself. You don't deceive anyone else. You deceive only yourself.

I ran into this problem very early in my training for the ministry. When I went to college as a freshman, my first roommate was a young man who was also studying for the ministry. He was a sweet boy in many ways. The only trouble with him was that he was *perfect*. When I found the room which had been assigned to me, my roommate was not at home, but when he came in, he introduced himself and informed me that he had not committed a sin in so many years—I have forgotten if he said one, two, or three years. It shocked me to meet a fellow who didn't sin. I had hoped he would be my buddy, but he wasn't a buddy. You see, in every room where I have lived, things go wrong once in a while. And there I was living in a room in which there were only two of us and one of us couldn't do anything wrong. So when something went wrong, guess who was to blame? Now I admit that *usually* it was my fault—but not *always*. Although he was a nice fellow, he hadn't reached the level of perfection which he claimed; he wasn't perfect. After the first semester, a freshman was permitted to move wherever he wished, so I told him, "I'm moving out." He was greatly distressed and said, "Oh, no! Where are you going?" I told him, "I have met a fellow down the hall who is just as mean as I am, and I'm going to move in with him." So I did move out, and I understand he didn't get a roommate after that. My new roommate and I got along wonderfully well. In fact, I still visit him down in the state of Florida. We are old men now and we still have wonderful times together. Neither of us is perfect although we have mellowed a bit down through the years.

My friend, if you feel that you have reached the state of perfection, I really feel sorry for your spouse because it is hard to live with someone who thinks he is perfect. John says, "If we say that we have no sin, we deceive ourselves, and the truth is not in us." We cannot bring ourselves up to God's level. It is impossible to reach perfection in this life.

Let me give you another instance of this because I think it is important. When I first came to Pasadena, I knew a man who served for a while as chaplain at the jail. He was a wonderful, enthusiastic Christian. I certainly had no criticism of him. But one day he met me on the street and said, "Brother Vernon, I got sanctified last night." I said, "You did! What really happened to you?" He told me that he had reached the place where he could no longer sin.

Well, I didn't see him for a while after that, but one of the officers of the church I served at the time lived next door to him. The son of the man who had reached perfection came to visit and parked his trailer in the back yard with part of it on the property of the man who was an officer in my church. He said nothing for a while, but the time came when he had to build a shed on that spot. The neighbor knew he was intending to do this, but he made no mention of it. Finally, when it looked as if the son was going to stay and he felt that he could wait no longer to build, he went to his neighbor and asked him to move the trailer. Well, the fellow lost his temper and really told him what kind of a neighbor he thought he was. The man who was the officer in my church casually mentioned the incident to me one day; so I couldn't wait to meet that fellow and finally I looked him up. I said to him, "Didn't you tell me that you got sanctified?"

"Yes."

"And when you got sanctified, you reached the plane of sinless perfection?"

"Yes, I think I have reached it."

"Well, your neighbor is a member of my church, and he tells me that you really lost your temper the other day and told him off in a very unkind, un-Christianlike manner."

He began to hem and haw. "I guess I did lose my temper. But that is not sin."

"Oh, if it's not sin, what is it?"

"I just made a mistake. I recognize that I shouldn't have done it—so that's not a sin."

"Well, I want you to shake hands with me now, because I've reached that plane, too. I don't sin; I just make mistakes—and I make a lot of them. But, brother, the Word of God will make it very clear to you that losing your temper and bawling out your neighbor as you did *is sin*."

My friend, whom do you think you deceive when you say that you have no sin? You deceive *yourself*, and you are the only person whom you do deceive. You don't deceive God. You don't deceive your neighbors. You don't deceive your friends. But you sure do deceive yourself. And John says that the truth is not in a man like that because he can't see that he is a sinner and that he has not reached the place of perfection. Yet a great many folk are trying that route in their effort to bridge the gap between themselves and a holy God.

Since you cannot bring God down to your level and you cannot bring yourself up to His level, what are you going to do? John gives us the alternative here—

If we confess our sins, he is faithful and just to forgive us our sins, and to cleanse us from all unrighteousness [1 John 1:9].

"If we confess our sins." Here is another one of our "if's." We have seen several of them: "If we say that we have fellowship" (v. 6); "If we walk in the light" (v. 7); and "If we say that we have no sin" (v. 8). Now here is the right method for bringing together a sinful man and a holy God: *confession of sins*.

What does it mean to confess our sins? The word *confess* is from the Greek verb *homologeō*, meaning "to say the same thing." *Logeō* means "to say" and *homo* means "the same." You are to say the same thing that God says. When God in His Word says that the thing you did is sin, you are to get over on God's side and look at it. And you are to say, "You are right, Lord, I say the same thing that You say. It is *sin*." That is what it means to confess your sins. That, my friend, is one of the greatest needs in the church. This is God's way for a Christian to deal with sin in his own life.

The other day I talked to a man who got into deep trouble. He divorced his wife—he found out that she had been unfaithful. He lost his home and lost his job. He was a very discouraged man. He said to me, "I want to serve God, and I have failed. I am a total failure." I very frankly said to him, "Don't cry on my shoulder. Go and tell God about it. He wants you to come to Him. Tell Him you have failed. Tell Him you have been wrong. Tell Him that you want to say the same thing about your sin that He says about it. Seek His help. He is your Father. You are in the family. You have lost your fellowship with Him, but you can have your fellowship restored. If you confess your sins, He is faithful and just to forgive you your sins."

After we confess our sins, what does God do? He *cleanses* us. In the parable, the Prodigal Son came home from the far country smelling like a pigpen. You don't think the father would have put a new robe on that ragged, dirty boy, smelling like that, do you? No, he gave him a good bath. The Roman world majored in cleanliness, and I am confident that the boy was bathed before that new robe was put on him. The next week he didn't say, "Dad, I think I will be going to the far country and end up in the pigpen again." Not that boy.

When you have confessed your sin, it means that you have turned from that sin. It means that you have said the same thing which God has said. Sin is a terrible thing. God hates it and now you hate it. But confession restores you to your Father.

John concludes this by saying—

If we say that we have not sinned, we make him a liar, and his word is not in us [1 John 1:10].

Now don't make God a liar. Why don't you go to the Lord, my friend, and just open your heart and talk to him as you talk to no one else. Tell Him your problems. Tell Him your sins. Tell Him your weakness. Confess it all to Him. And say to your Father that you want to have fellowship with Him and you want to serve Him. My, He has made a marvelous, wonderful way back to Himself!

CHAPTER 2

THEME: The advocacy of Christ; how the dear children may have fellowship with each other; the "dear children" must not love the world

This chapter is a continuation of the thought begun in the previous chapter regarding the manner in which "little children" may have fellowship with God. We have seen that we can have fellowship with God by walking in the light, that is, in God's presence. The second thing we must do in order to maintain that fellowship is to confess our sins to Him. When we walk in the light, we know that the blood of Jesus Christ keeps on cleansing us from all sin, but we also know that there is imperfection in our lives and that we must go to Him in confession.

In chapter 2 we come to the matter of the advocacy of Christ. We will now see the conclusion of that which began with 1 John 1:5, where John said, "This then is the message." What is the message? It is the message of the gospel of the grace of God that takes the hell-doomed sinner and by simple faith in Christ brings him into the family of God where he becomes an heir and joint-heir with Jesus Christ. It is the relationship with the Father that is all important.

FELLOWSHIP WITH GOD BY THE ADVOCACY OF CHRIST

My little children, these things write I unto you, that ye sin not. And if any man sin, we have an advocate with the Father, Jesus Christ the righteous [1 John 2:1].

"My little children, these things write I unto you, that ye sin not." John is writing these things to us because God does not want His children to sin. Although God has made ample and adequate provision for us not to sin, our entrance into His provision is imperfect—because of our imperfection. Notice that this verse does not say that we *cannot* sin, but John is writing to us that we *may* not sin. God wants us to walk in a manner that is well pleasing to Him; that is, He wants us to walk in obedience to His Word.

Let me remind you that 1 John is a *family* epistle; it emphasizes the relationship of the family of God. I mention this again because there is so much emphasis in the contemporary church on "body" truth; that is, that all believers are part of a body. "Body" truth is the message of Ephesians, and it is wonderful, but now we need to move out a little farther into "family" truth. We need to recognize that we are in God's family and that our relationship is all important. We need to have *fellowship* with our heavenly Father.

"My little children" is an interesting expression. It comes from the Greek word *teknia* and probably should be translated "my little born ones" or "my little born-again ones." I like the Scottish term best, "my little bairns."

"These things write I unto you, that ye sin not." None of us has reached that exalted plane, although there are those who claim sinless perfection. I am reminded of an occasion when a speaker was emphasizing the fact that nobody is perfect. Finally he became very dramatic and oratorical and asked, "Is there anybody here who has ever seen a perfect man?" No one responded until one little fellow in the back of the auditorium, sort of a Mr. Milquetoast, put up his hand.

The speaker asked, "Have *you* seen a perfect man?"

The little fellow stood to his feet and said, "Well, I have never *seen* him, but I have *heard* about him."

"Who is he?"

"He is my wife's first husband."

Well, I imagine he had heard about him a great deal! But the truth is that none of us has reached that exalted position of perfection.

Several years ago a speaker was telling a story about a family that was going to take a trip for a couple of days. They did not want to take their little girl along, so they left her with neighbors, who had four boys. When they returned, the little girl said to her daddy, "There are four boys in that house where I have been staying. They have family worship there every night. Each night their father prays for his four little boys."

Her father replied, "That certainly is good to hear."

"Daddy, he prays that God will make them good boys, and he prays that they won't do anything wrong."

Her father said, "Well, that's very fine."

The little girl was silent for a moment, and then she added, "But, Daddy, He hasn't done it yet."

If we are honest with ourselves, we too will have to say that God hasn't made us perfect yet either. We have not reached that exalted plane of sinless perfection. John says, "My little born ones, my little bairns, I write these things unto you that you may not be sinning." God doesn't want you to live in sin. We are going to find later that John is going to say, "Whosoever is born of God sinneth not" (1 John 5:18). This means that whosoever is born of God does not *practice* sin; that is, *live* in sin. The prodigal son got up out of the pigpen and went home to his father. He did not stay in the pigpen. Why not? Because he was a son and not a pig. Also we need to realize, as it is stated in Ecclesiastes 7:20, "For there is not a just man upon earth, that doeth good, and sinneth not."

Today you and I may be able to say, "I don't think I have done anything real bad." But how about doing good? James says, "Therefore to him that knoweth to do good, and doeth it not, to him it is sin" (James 4:17). There are sins of commission and sins of omission. You and I are to walk in the light. When we walk in the light, we will see just how far we have fallen short of what God wants. Every sincere child of God wants to have fellowship with Him, and yet he knows within himself that he has fallen far short of the kind of life he should have. There is sin in his life, and sin, be it ever so small, breaks communion with the Father.

It is said of Spurgeon that when he was crossing a street one day, he suddenly stopped. It looked like he was praying, and he was. One of his deacons waited for him on the other side of the street and said to him, "You could have been run down by a carriage [this was before the day of the automobile]. What were you doing? It looked like you were praying."

Spurgeon replied, "I was praying."

The deacon then asked, "Was it so important?"

"Indeed it was. A cloud came between me and my Savior, and I wanted to remove it even before I got across the street."

Many Christians are living lives in which they are constantly disobeying God, yet they wonder why they aren't having fellowship with Him. They need to recognize that sin causes a break in fellowship.

They need to know that they have not lost their salvation, because in the next breath John adds, "If any man sin, we have an advocate with the Father, Jesus Christ the righteous." Notice that John says, "We have an advocate with the Father"—John doesn't call Him by the impersonal name *God* because He is still our *Father* even though we have sinned. Therefore we need to recognize that our salvation rests upon what Christ has done for us, and that is a finished work. Someone has expressed it like this:

> Upon a life I did not live,
>   Upon a death I did not die,
> Another's life, Another's death,
>   I stake my whole eternity.
>
> It is finished, yes, indeed;
>   Finished, every jot!
> Sinner, this is all you need!
>   Tell me, is it not?
>   —Author unknown

We cannot add anything to a finished work. What Christ has done is all we need for salvation.

However, if you and I are going to have fellowship with Him, we need to recognize something else.

"And if any man sin, we have an advocate with the Father." Who is He? He is "Jesus Christ the righteous." The word *advocate* is from the Greek *paraklētos,* the same word which is translated "comforter" in John's Gospel. The Holy Spirit is our Comforter down here, and Christ is our Comforter up there.

Advocate—a paraclete, a helper—is a legal term. It means "one who will come to your side to help in every time of need." We have a wonderful heavenly Father, and we don't lose our salvation when we sin, but there is somebody up there who wants us to lose it, and that is Satan. Satan is the accuser of the brethren. In Revelation 12:10 we are told that he accuses us before our God day and night. Satan is there at the throne of God accusing you and accusing me. Remember how he accused Job. In effect, he said to God, "If you will let me get to him, I'll show You that he will curse you." When that happens in our case, the Lord Jesus is able to step in as our Advocate. He died *for* us! Yet the accuser is there, and some folk are very disturbed by that. But the Advocate is far greater than the accuser. Someone has expressed this in beautiful poetic language:

> I hear the accuser roar
> Of ills that I have done;
> I know them well, and thousands more,
> Jehovah findeth none.
>
> Though the restless foe accuses—
> Sins recounting like a flood,
> Ev'ry charge our God refuses;
> Christ has answered with His blood.
> —Author unknown

And he is the propitiation for our sins: and not for ours only, but also for the sins of the whole world [1 John 2:2].

"And he is the propitiation for our sins." The word *propitiation*, as it is used here in John's epistle, is a different word from that used in the Epistle to the Romans. In Romans the meaning is "mercy seat"— Christ is the propitiation, the mercy seat, the meeting place between God and man. However, here in 1 John *propitiation* means "an atonement or an expiation." It means that sins have been paid for by the suffering of Another. Christ is my Advocate, interceding for me, and He Himself is the propitiation.

Notice that John does not say that if anyone *repents*, he has an Advocate nor if anyone confesses his sins, he has an Advocate. Neither does he say that if anyone goes through a ceremony to get rid of his sins, he has an Advocate. What he does say is that if any man *sin*, we have an Advocate with the Father. Before we even repent of that cruel or brutal word we said, the very moment we had that evil thought, and the moment we did that wrong act, Jesus Christ was there at the throne of God to represent us as Satan was there accusing us.

Then, because of the faithful advocacy of Christ, the Holy Spirit brings conviction to us, and we confess our sin to the Father. As we said before, to confess means that we get on God's side and we see our sin from His viewpoint and confess that it *is* sin.

The sincere child of God wants to please the Father, and he walks along with that in mind. The psalmist expressed it this way: "Search me, O God, and know my heart: try me, and know my thoughts: And see if there be any wicked way in me, and lead me in the way everlasting" (Ps. 139:23–24).

Dr. Harry Ironside has illustrated the confession that God requires with an incident in his own home. He had trouble one evening with one of his boys, so he sent the boy upstairs and told him not to come down to supper until he confessed the thing he had done wrong. The boy would not admit anything at all. Finally the boy called for Dr. Ironside to come upstairs and asked if he could go down to supper. His father said, "It depends upon you." The boy said, "If you think I have done something wrong, I am sorry." His father said, "That won't do." Later the boy called him upstairs again, and this time he changed his story a little. He said. "Well, since you and mother both think I have done something wrong, I guess I have. I want to come down to supper." Once again his father told him that that wasn't good enough. Dr. Ironside went downstairs, and later on he heard the boy almost weeping. He said, "Dad, please forgive me. I know I have done wrong. Please forgive me." Then the lad came downstairs, and the family had a wonderful supper together because fellowship had been restored.

My friend, if you are a child of God, you are in the *family* of God, and He wants to have *fellowship* with you. I don't care about these little rules you are following. You think that some way you are going to be able to live the Christian life by following rules. My friend, God doesn't want you to be a programmed computer. He is not trying to do that to you. You are a human being with your own free will, but you are a member of His family, and He wants to have fellowship with you. We can talk to Him like we can talk to no one else.

Up to this point, John's subject has been that God is light and how God's dear children may have fellowship with Him. Now in this second section, the subject is that God is love and how God's dear children may have fellowship with each other. Before, he was talking about walking in *light*; now he will be talking about walking in *love*. Love is the very heart of this epistle. The word occurs thirty-three times, and there is a great emphasis upon it.

HOW TO HAVE FELLOWSHIP WITH EACH OTHER

And hereby we do know that we know him, if we keep his commandments [1 John 2:3].

First of all, let me point out that this verse has nothing to do with the security of the believer. John is talking about assurance. As God's children, we are in a family. But how can we have the assurance that we are in God's family? He is telling us that assurance comes by keeping His commandments.

"If we keep his commandments" does not refer to the Ten Commandments. John is not dealing with any legal aspects; he is dealing with family matters. The Ten Commandments were given to a nation, and on these commandments every civilized nation has based its laws. The Ten Commandments are for the unsaved. Now God has something for His own family, and they are commandments for His children. For example, in Galatians 6:2 the family is told, "Bear ye one another's burdens, and so fulfil the law of Christ." In 1 Thessalonians 4:2 Paul tells the family of Christ, "For ye know what commandments we gave you by the Lord Jesus." Some of those commandments are mentioned in the last chapter of 1 Thessalonians. I have counted twenty-two commandments in that chapter, and here are a few of them. "Rejoice evermore"—God wants you to be a joyful Christian. "Pray without ceasing" refers to an *attitude* of prayer. That is, when you get off your knees, you still are to walk in a prayerful attitude. "Quench not the Spirit"—don't say no to Him. These are some of the commandments which the Lord Jesus has given to believers, and if we are to have fellowship with the Father and enjoy it by having assurance in our own hearts, we must keep His commandments. We do not feel that we are free to do as we please. The Christian doesn't do as *he* pleases; he does as *Christ* pleases.

"And hereby we do know that we know him." Remember that throughout this epistle John is answering the Gnostics who claimed to have a superior knowledge that no one else had—and generally it was heresy. The apostle John is saying that the important thing is to know Jesus Christ. And how can we have the assurance that we know Him? My friend, although a great many folk believe in the security of the believer, they don't have the assurance of salvation, and the reason is obvious. We cannot know that we are children of God if we are disobedient to Him. Obedience to Christ is essential and is the very basis of assurance. You cannot have that assurance (oh, you can bluff your way through, but you cannot have that deep, down-in-your-heart assurance) unless you keep His commandments.

> **He that saith, I know him, and keepeth not his commandments, is a liar, and the truth is not in him [1 John 2:4].**

I would call this very plain talk! In the previous verse John has said that we *know* that we *know* Him—this is the positive side. We know by experience in contrast to the esoteric knowledge of the Gnostics. Now he presents the negative side: disobedience to Christ is a proof that we do not know Him. This is plain and direct language. Disobedience to Christ on the part of a professing Christian is tantamount to being a liar. In other words, his life is a lie.

There are a great many people who say they are children of God, but are they? It is one thing to *say* you are a child of God, and it is another thing to be a possessor of eternal life, to have a new nature that cries out to the Father for fellowship and wants to obey Him. You cannot make me believe that all of these church members who have no love for the Word of God and are disobedient to Christ are really His children. I do not believe they have had the experience of regeneration. John is making it very clear that we know that we know Him because we keep His commandments.

Let me repeat that John is *not* talking about the Ten Commandments that were given to the nation Israel in the Old Testament. John is talking about the commandments that Christ gave to the church. If a child of God does not have a love for these commandments, he is in the very gall of bitterness and in the bond of iniquity, as the Scripture says (see Acts 8:23).

The Lord Jesus, when He was here in the flesh, said of the Father, ". . . I do always those things that please him" (John 8:29). I can't say that, but I can say that I *want* to please Him, and I have dedicated my life to that end. Although I sometimes stumble and fall, I *want* to please Him. While it is true that "he that believeth on the Son hath everlasting life . . ." (John 3:36), it corroborates his faith when in his heart he knows that he wants to do God's will. The natural man never did want to do God's will. Oh, boy, this is a strong statement which John makes! "He that saith, I know him, and keepeth not his commandments, is a liar, and the truth is not in him." And John will tell us that the Holy Spirit is the one who prompted him to say it. The truth is not in a man who claims to be a child of God but does not keep His commandments.

> **But whoso keepeth his word, in him verily is the love of God perfected: hereby know we that we are in him [1 John 2:5].**

I want to make a distinction that I find very few expositors make. Even *The Scofield Reference Bible* does not make this distinction. I feel there is a difference between the Word of God and the *commandments* of God. Somebody is going to call my attention to the fact that the commandments are the Word of God. Well, commandments are the Word of God, but the Word of God is not all commandments. It is more than that. I hope you see the distinction. There are commandments in the Word of God, but the Word of God is not only commandments. The Word is the expression of the will of God, either by commandment or otherwise. In the Word of God you have His complete revelation to us about His will for our lives.

In John 14:15 the Lord made this statement: "If ye love me, keep my commandments." In John 14:23 He said, ". . . If a man love me, he will keep my words. . . ." What is the distinction here? Let me illustrate this. Suppose the home of a young boy is in the country. His father is a farmer. One day, when the boy is on his way to school, his father says, "Son, I'll milk the cow when I come in from the field each day, but when you get home from school, I want you to chop wood, put it on the back porch, and tell your mama so she can make a fire in the cook stove and in the fireplace." When the boy comes home, he obeys his father's commandment that he chop wood. He spends about an hour and a half chopping wood after school, and he stacks it on the back porch. Then one morning at the breakfast table, the father says, "I don't feel well today. I feel so bad that I don't think I can go out and work in the field today." But he goes out anyway. Now when the boy comes home from school, although his only commandment is to chop wood, he knows that his father is sick and doesn't feel like milking the cow, so he not only chops the wood but he milks the cow also. He chops the wood because he was commanded to do so, but he milks the cow because he loves his father.

In just this way a child of God not only wants to obey the commandments of God but he also wants to obey the Word of God. He wants to please his Father in everything that he does. I get the impression from many folk that they want to live as much like the unsaved as possible and still be Christians. I would never give an answer to a young person who asked me if a Christian could do this or that and still be a Christian—because they were asking the wrong questions. The right question to ask is this: "What can I do to please my heavenly Father?" You see, a genuine child of God wants to please Him; he does not try to live right on the margin of the Christian life.

There are many Christians in our day who feel that they need to be broad-minded. They are against whiskey, but they use beer and they use wine, which gives them the feeling of being broad-minded. And, of course, they feel that I am very narrow-minded. Well, it is not a question of a thing being right or wrong—I hope you are above that plane, my Christian friend—the question is: does it please my heavenly Father? I want to do the thing that will please Him, bring joy to His heart and fellowship and joy to my own life. All of this, you see, is on the basis of love: "If you love me, keep my commandments," and "If a man love me, he will keep my words." If you love Him, you will do more than keep His commandments; you will do something extra for Him.

I feel that a great many folk have in their thinking only the sins of commission and forget about the sins of omission. James said, ". . . to him that knoweth to do good, and doeth it not, to him it is sin" (James 4:17). There are many things I know I should do, but I neglect to do them. These are sins of omission. The Bible makes no distinction between the gravity of sins of commission and sins of omission. They are equally bad.

My friend, verse 5 is very important. Let me repeat it: "But whoso keepeth his word, in him verily is the love of God perfected [that is, realized in practice]: hereby [by this] know we that we are in him." When the love of God is perfected in you, it means that you have passed the commandments and you just want to please God.

I suggest that you take an inventory of yourself. What is your attitude toward sin? Does it trouble you? Does it break your fellowship with the Father? Does it cause you to cry out in the night, "Oh, God, I'm wrong, and I want to confess the wrong I have done. I want fellowship with You." On that basis God will restore fellowship with us, and the assurance of salvation comes to our hearts.

He that saith he abideth in him ought himself also so to walk, even as he walked [1 John 2:6].

We cannot do or be all that the Lord Jesus Christ did or was, but if we set our hearts on doing our Father's will, which was the thing that the Lord Jesus put uppermost in His life, then we are walking as (in the same manner as) He walked.

I hear the word *commitment* a great deal these days. When an invitation is given after a message, the question is asked, "Do you want to commit your life to Christ?" What do they mean by that? Well, let me tell you what John means by full commitment. It is to love Christ. And if you love Christ, you are going to keep His Word—you can't help it. You *want* to please the person you love. You don't want to offend; you want to please. This is the reason I send a dozen American Beauty roses to my wife occasionally. You see, the question is not "Are you committed to Christ?" The question is, "Do you love Christ?"

> **Brethren, I write no new commandment unto you, but an old commandment which ye had from the beginning. The old commandment is the word which ye have heard from the beginning [1 John 2:7].**

"An old commandment which ye had from the beginning." From what beginning? Well, the "beginning" in 1 John is the incarnation of Christ. It began in Bethlehem, then worked itself out in a carpenter shop and three years of public ministry. The "commandment which ye had from the beginning" was what the Lord Jesus gave to His apostles when He was with them on earth—which He repeated many times. For example, in John 13:34–35 we read, "A new commandment I give unto you, That ye love one another; as I have loved you, that ye also love one another. By this shall all men know that ye are my disciples, if ye have love one to another." And in John 15:10, 12, "If ye keep my commandments, ye shall abide in my love; even as I have kept my Father's commandments, and abide in his love. . . . This is my commandment, That ye love one another, as I have loved you."

John is saying, "This old commandment is what I am giving to you. It is what the Lord Jesus said when He taught here upon this earth." Then John continues—

> **Again, a new commandment I write unto you, which thing is true in him and in you: because the darkness is past, and the true light now shineth [1 John 2:8].**

Now, why is it a new commandment for believers who are regenerated and indwelt by the Holy Spirit? Because it was given on the other side of the Cross, before the coming of the Holy Spirit. On this side it is *new*.

Believers are to do the will of God; and the will of God, first of all, is to love Him. This identifies a believer. A believer is one who delights to do the will of God. Because "the darkness is past, and the true light now shineth," the believer ought to be able to say that he is getting to know the Lord God better and that he is understanding His will more perfectly. Schiller, the great German poet, said, "I see everything clearer and clearer." And that should be the experience of every child of God. Every day we should be growing, and it is impossible to grow apart from a study of the Word of God. The written Word reveals the living Word, the Lord Jesus Christ, and He is the Bread of Life and the Water of Life. We will famish if we don't feed upon Him.

Let me repeat that the great problem in the world today is that the majority of believers are trying to follow a few little rules and regulations; they are programmed like a computer. They feel that they are living the Christian life if they do all those little things. Oh, my friend, you are not a computer; you are a human being. If you are a child of God, you have a new nature—although you still have your old nature in which ". . . dwelleth no good thing . . ." (Rom. 7:18). But your new nature wants to do God's will; it wants to please Him.

"The darkness is past, and the true light now shineth" would be better translated, "the darkness is passing." As you look around you today, you will see that the darkness has not passed yet. Ignorance of the Word of God is still much in evidence. The "true light," who is the Lord Jesus Christ, is breaking upon this world. He still is the most controversial person who has ever lived on the earth.

He that saith he is in the light, and hateth his brother, is in darkness even until now [1 John 2:9].

It is impossible for you as a child of God to walk in the light and hate your brother. If you do hate another Christian, it means there is something radically wrong with your confession of faith. This doesn't mean that there are not some people whose manners and habits will be objectionable to you. This doesn't mean that there won't be some believers who have certain habits that you don't approve of—that is understandable. But to *hate* them reveals that you are in darkness. Hatred of a fellow believer is evidence that a person is not in the light. This is something we need to keep in mind. There is the natural darkness in which all men are born. Paul talks about it in Ephesians 4:18, where he says, "Having the understanding darkened, being alienated from the life of God through the ignorance that is in them, because of the blindness of their heart." That is the condition of mankind by nature. But our condemnation is not because of what we are by nature. "And this is the condemnation, that light is come into the world, and men loved darkness rather than light, because their deeds were evil" (John 3:19). This is important. Don't let it slip by you. We are not responsible because we are sinners by nature; we are responsible if we reject the Savior. We are not responsible because we were born in darkness and because our understanding is darkened; we are responsible if we reject the light that comes to us through the Word of God.

If you walk in the light, it will chase away all darkness. Instead of turning from its searching rays, let it search your heart. If a man keeps on rejecting this light, there will come a day when God will withdraw the light altogether. Or that man will become sunburned. Esau was that kind of man. He was red. He was sunburned. He was not only sunburned physically, he was also sunburned spiritually. What is sunburn? It means the skin will absorb all the rays of the light except one particular ray, and that is what burns. The soul that will not accept the Lord Jesus Christ as Savior, the Light of the World, will become sunburned, just as Esau was.

John gives us a test to see if we are in darkness. This is the test—

He that loveth his brother abideth in the light, and there is none occasion of stumbling in him.

But he that hateth his brother is in darkness, and walketh in darkness, and knoweth not whither he goeth, because that darkness hath blinded his eyes [1 John 2:10–11].

When the Lord Jesus was here on earth, He said, ". . . I am the light of the world: he that followeth me shall not walk in darkness, but shall have the light of life" (John 8:12). My friend, we need to apply John's test to our own lives. Have you really trusted Christ? Is He your light? Is He the one who is so guiding you that you are not hating your brother?

Here is a bit of poetry which sets this truth before us—

> I heard the voice of Jesus say,
>   "I am this world's light.
> Look unto Me, thy morn shall rise,
>   And all thy days be bright."
>
> I looked to Jesus, and I found
>   In Him my star, my sun,
> And in that light of life I'll walk,
>   Till traveling days are done.
>
> "I Heard the Voice of Jesus Say"
> —Horatius Bonar

Now, of course, there are other believers whose habits you dislike. You may have a distaste for some of their expressions. You may even have a personality that clashes with that of another brother. But that doesn't mean you hate him.

When I was attending seminary, I roomed with a fellow who had some of the meanest habits I have ever seen in a Christian. He would start singing at night after I went to bed and was asleep. He wouldn't sing all day long, but at eleven o'clock at night, he was ready to tune up. He had a lot of mean habits like that. So one day I told him, "You know, you are the greatest proof to me that I am a child of God." He asked, "What do you mean?" I replied, "You are the most nauseating, the most sickening Christian that I have ever met, but I do want you to know something—I love you." He looked right at me and said, "I want you to know that you are the most abominable Christian I have ever met, and I also want you to know you are the hardest person in the world to love, but I love you." Years later that fellow got into some trouble. I made a trip to see him, to see if there was anything I could do to help him. When I met him, I found that he wasn't any more lovable than he had been when I roomed with him. He was even more objectionable, and I think he found me the same, but I didn't hate him. That man was a child of God, and God marvelously used him in the ministry. In many ways he was a great fellow. I don't know why it is that when a Christian finds he doesn't like somebody, he thinks the only alternative is to hate him. You don't have to hate him at all; you are to love him as a child of God.

My friend, John has given here a tremendous statement: "He that hateth his brother is in darkness, and walketh in darkness, and knoweth not whither he goeth, because that darkness hath blinded his eyes." If you want to know for sure that you are a child of God, apply this test to your own life. If you are hating your brother, you are dwelling in darkness. If you are loving your brother, you are dwelling in light.

The Christian life is like a triangle. Let me diagram it for you (see below). God is at the top of the triangle, and the light of God comes down into your heart and life. Your love for God goes up, for you love Him because He first loved you. If you are walking in the light down here, it means you are going to love your brother also. You cannot say you love God and hate your brother. That is absolutely impossible, and John will make this very clear later on.

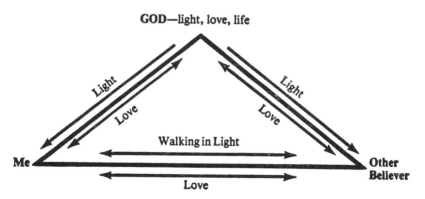

GOD—light, love, life

Light   Light
Love   Love

Walking in Light

Me   Other
                      Believer

Love

At this point it seems to me that we have a departure from the theme which John has been following. He begins to talk about the three different degrees of believers.

> **I write unto you, little children, because your sins are forgiven you for his name's sake [1 John 2:12].**

These whom he calls "little children," the Greek *teknia*, little born ones, I think refer to all believers, regardless of their age or their maturity as believers. The basis on which all Christians rest is the forgiveness of sins because of the shed blood of Christ. "Your sins are forgiven you for his name's sake."

Some Christians stay in that position of little children and never move out of that area.

Now John moves to another group—

> **I write unto you, fathers, because ye have known him that is from the beginning. I write unto you, young men, because ye have overcome the wicked one. I write unto you, little children, because ye have known the Father [1 John 2:13].**

"Fathers" are the saints who have known the Lord Jesus for many years and have grown and matured. Personally, I think that David wrote Psalm 23 when he was an old man. He could never have written that psalm as a young shepherd, because it is a psalm which had grown out of life's vicissitudes. David had faced all sorts of problems and dangers, and he had lived in fellowship with God. He was a matured child of God and would certainly fall under John's classification of "fathers." I have called Psalm 23 the psalm of an old king. I believe David wrote it as he was seated upon his throne, looking back over his life. He remembers that shepherd boy who would take the flocks out to pasture on the hills of Bethlehem, how he would protect them from the bears and lions. Then he remembers when he was made king and became the shepherd of a people. As he looks back over his checkered career, he recalls his wonderful friendship with Jonathan, his flight from King Saul, then his reign in Hebron, and finally when God made him king over all twelve tribes. Then he remembers his awful sin and God's gracious forgiveness when he confessed it to Him. He recalls the trouble in his home (because God had taken him to the woodshed), especially the rebellion of Absalom, the son whom he most loved. He recalls his flight from Jerusalem and being holed up again and then receiving the news of Absalom's death, which had been a heartbreak to him. With these things in mind, the old king says, "The Lord is my shepherd; I shall not want" (Ps. 23:1). As a mature child of God, he recounts how God led him in green pastures and beside still waters and restored his soul. It is folk like David whom John is addressing as "fathers."

"I write unto you, young men, because ye have overcome the wicked one." The "young men" are not as mature as the fathers, that is, they haven't had the experience the fathers have had, but they have learned the secret of overcoming the enemy by the blood of Christ. They have learned how to live for God. Don't tell me that a young person cannot live for God in this day.

"I write unto you, little children, because ye have known the Father." The "little children" in this case is the Greek *paidia*, immature little folk. They are the ones who know they are the children of God, but that is about all they know—and some of them feel that is all they want to know. Oh, how many children of God fall into this classification! In some churches you feel as if you are in a spiritual nursery! Although the folk are physically full-grown, some of them with gray hair, they are still spiritually immature. They never did grow up.

Now John has something more to add; so he goes over each of these degrees of believers again.

I have written unto you, fathers, because ye have known him that is from the beginning. I have written unto you, young men, because ye are strong, and the word of God abideth in you, and ye have overcome the wicked one [1 John 2:14].

"I have written unto you, fathers, because ye have known him that is from the beginning." John doesn't add anything to that because you can't go beyond that. As Paul expressed it, knowing ". . . him, and the power of his resurrection, and the fellowship of his sufferings, being made conformable unto his death" (Phil. 3:10) is what makes one a father in Christ.

My friend, how do you get to know somebody? By living with him day by day. I have discovered that my wife knows me. She has been living with me for over forty years so she knows me very well. And the summer I was forced to stay home because of illness, she and I sat on our back patio and really got acquainted with each other. We talked about many things from the time we met down to the present. Although I was sick during that time, it was the greatest summer I have ever spent. I know her better now, and she knows me better.

Now how are we going to know the Lord Jesus Christ? My friend, the only way you can know Him is in the Word of God. That is where He is revealed. Many folk feel that if they go to a Bible study once a week, they will become super-duper saints. But the Word of God is like food. I've conducted Bible studies once a week over the years, and I certainly approve of them, but imagine going in and eating a good meal and then saying, "I'll be back for another meal in a week." Well, if you don't get any food in the meantime, you will be in bad shape. This is the reason I have maintained a *daily* Bible-teaching program by radio. The Word of God is the Bread of Life. If we are to know Christ, we must live with Him in His Word as we go through the joys and sorrows of this life.

Now John addresses the second group—"I have written unto you, young men, because ye are strong, and the word of God abideth in you, and ye have overcome the wicked one." In the previous verse John said that the young men were strong and they were able to overcome the wicked one. But now he gives the secret: "the word of God abideth in you." My friend, how can you and I overcome the wicked one? With the Word of God. In Ephesians 6 the Christian's armor is listed, piece by piece, and the weapon of offense is the ". . . sword of the Spirit, which is the word of God" (Eph. 6:17). If you are going to be able to defend yourself against the Devil, you will have to have a good knowledge of the Word of God. The reason so many believers are succumbing to the sins of the world is that they are not studying the Word of God. You eat three times a day—you need physical food to be strong—and, believe me, you need spiritual food to be strong also.

DEAR CHILDREN MUST NOT LOVE THE WORLD

This is a section which a great many would separate from what has gone before, but I feel that it is very much a part of what John has been talking about. John has been telling us how we as God's children can know that we are His children. He has said that the way we can know is by the fact that we love Him and keep His commandments. Later on, John is going to say that His commandments are not grievous. We are not talking about the Ten Commandments here but about the commandments which the Lord Jesus gave, for we have been brought into the Holy of Holies in a very personal relationship with the Lord Jesus Christ. Someone has made this division which I like: The Epistle to the Romans deals with how we come out of the house of bondage; Ephesians is how we enter the banqueting house; Hebrews is how we approach the throne of grace, but 1 John is how we approach the divine presence.

The way in which we can have assurance and be a proof not only to our neighbor but also to ourselves that we are genuine children of God is by our obedience to Him and our desire to please Him in all we do. I feel that there are some folk today who more or less grit their teeth and say, "Yes, I'll obey Him." But their motive is not love, and love should be the motive for obedience to Him. The Lord Jesus said, "If ye love me, keep my commandments" (John 14:15).

My friend, when you obey the commandments of Christ because you love Him, a great many of the family problems will be solved and a great deal of the uncertainty in your own heart will disappear. If someone is offering a little course to follow in living the Christian life, people come running. A great many folk like to lean on something— even if it is a poor, broken reed which won't hold them up.

Christianity is based on a love relationship. Salvation is a love affair. John is going to tell us more about this later when he says, "We love him, because he first loved us" (1 John 4:19).

> **Love not the world, neither the things that are in the world. If any man love the world, the love of the Father is not in him [1 John 2:15].**

"Love not the world, neither the things that are in the world." What "world" is John talking about? He does not mean the world of creation, that is, the system and order found in the physical creation. In spring the flowers bloom and the trees put out leaves. In the fall the leaves begin to turn all kinds of beautiful colors, like yellow and gold and red. Then the leaves fall off, and winter soon comes. This is not the world we are warned against loving. This is the world God created for our enjoyment.

It is just as the poet says in "The Vision of Sir Launfal"—

> And what is so rare as a day in June?
>   Then, if ever, come perfect days;
> Then Heaven tries earth if it be in tune,
>   And over it softly her warm ear lays;
> Whether we look, or whether we listen,
> We hear life murmur, or see it glisten.

> —James Russell Lowell

I learned that poem when I was in grammar school, and it has always stayed with me. My birthday is in June, and in June I always think of how wonderful nature is.

The hymn writer has put it like this—

> Heav'n above is softer blue,
>   Earth around is sweeter green!
> Something lives in every hue
>   Christless eyes have never seen:

Birds with gladder songs o'erflow,
Flow'rs with deeper beauties
shine,
Since I know, as now I know,
I am His, and He is mine.

"I Am His, and He Is Mine"
—Wade Robinson

Isn't that lovely? John is not talking about the physical earth where beautiful roses and tall trees grow. The wonderful mountains and the falls and the running streams are not what we are to hate. Rather, they are something we can admire and relish and enjoy.

Nor is the world about which John speaks the world of humanity or mankind. We are told that "God so *loved* the world." What world? The world of people, of human beings. ". . . God so loved the world, that he gave his only begotten Son . . ." (John 3:16).

Then what world does John mean? The Greek word for "world" here is *kosmos*. It means the world system, the organized system headed by Satan which leaves God out and is actually in opposition to Him. The thing which we need to hate today is this thing in the world which is organized against God.

Believe me, there is a world system in operation today, and it is satanic. John mentions this in his Gospel where the Lord Jesus says, "Hereafter I will not talk much with you: for the prince of this world cometh, and hath nothing in me" (John 14:30). "The prince of this world"—the prince of the world system, which is included in the civilization that you and I are in today. The world system belongs to Satan. He offered the kingdoms of this world to the Lord Jesus, and I don't think he left out the United States when he made the offer—it all belongs to him, and we are not to love this world. We read in John 16:11, "Of judgment, because the prince of this world is judged." Again, the Lord Jesus is referring to the satanic system that is in this world today. In Ephesians 1:4, when Paul speaks of ". . . the foundation of the world . . .", he is talking about the material creation, but when we come to Ephesians 2:2, he says, "Wherein in time past ye walked according to the course of this world. . . ." What is "the course of this world"? This is a world that is filled with greed, with selfish ambition, with fleshly pleasures, with deceit, and lying and danger. That is the world we live in, and John says that we are not to love the world. We are living in a godless world that is in rebellion against God. Our contemporary culture and civilization is anti-God, and the child of God ought not to love it. We are in the world, but we are not of the world. Many of us must move in the business world, many of us must move even in the social realm, but we do not have to be a part of it.

We need to recognize that we are going to be obedient to one world or the other. You are either going to obey the world system and live in it and enjoy it, or you are going to obey God. Listen to Paul in Galatians 6:14: "But God forbid that I should glory, save in the cross of our Lord Jesus Christ, by whom the world is crucified unto me, and I unto the world." In effect Paul is saying, "There stands between me and this satanic world system, a cross. Both are bidding for me and, as a child of God, I am obedient unto Him, and I glory in the Cross of Christ." You can be sure that the world today is not glorying in the Cross of Christ!

Peter also speaks of this: "For if after they have escaped the *pollutions* of the world . . ." (2 Pet. 2:20, italics mine). He spoke earlier of the *corruption* of the world. We live in a world that is corrupted and polluted. We are hearing so much today about air pollution and water pollution, but what about the minds which are being polluted by all the pornography and vile language? What about the spirit of man that is being dulled by all these things?

"If any man love the world, the love of the Father is not in him." You may run with the Devil's crowd all week long and then run with the Lord's crowd on Sunday, but it is obvious that the love of the Father is not in you.

In Romans 7 Paul describes his own struggle as a Christian. He says in effect, "I have discovered that in my flesh dwelleth no good thing. I have found that there is no power in the new nature. What I would not do, I'm doing. What the new nature wants to do, the old nature balks at—the old nature backslides and will not do that thing."

So there is a real conflict which goes on in the heart of the Christian as long as he is in the world with that old nature. For the old nature is geared to this world in which we live; it's meshed into the program of the world.

For all that is in the world, the lust of the flesh, and the lust of the eyes, and the pride of life, is not of the Father, but is of the world [1 John 2:16].

John lists these three things that are in the world. These are not only the temptations which face us, they are also the temptations which Satan brought to Eve (see Gen. 3:6) and to the Lord Jesus Christ (see Matt. 4:1–11).

1. *"The lust of the flesh."* Eve saw that the tree was good for food—if you were hungry, it was a good place to eat. Scripture condemns gluttony and the many other sins of the flesh. So many things appeal to the flesh. There is an overemphasis on sex today both in the church and out of the church—it is all of the flesh. Satan brought this same temptation to the Lord Jesus: "And when he had fasted forty days and forty nights, he was afterward an hungered. And when the tempter came to him, he said, If thou be the Son of God, command that these stones be made bread" (Matt. 4:2–3). The Lord Jesus could have done that. The difference between the Lord Jesus Christ and myself is that if I could turn stones into bread, I suspect that I would be doing it, but He didn't. He was being tested in that same area in which you and I are being tested—the desires of the flesh. We *are* being tested, and there is no sin in being tested. The sin is in yielding to the temptation. This same principle applies to sex or to any other realm of the desires of the flesh.

2. *"The lust of the eyes."* Eve saw that the tree was pleasant to the eyes. Remember also that Satan showed the Lord Jesus Christ all the kingdoms of this world. Let me tell you, they are very attractive, and they *are* in the hands of Satan. There is a godless philosophy which is trying to get control of the world today. There will come a day when

Antichrist will arise—he is coming to rule this world for Satan. This is an attractive world that we live in, with all of its display, all of its pageantry, all of its human glory.

3. *"The pride of life."* Eve saw that the tree was to be desired to make one wise. Many people like to pride themselves on their family. They pride themselves on the fact that they come from a very old family and upon the fact that they belong to a certain race. There are a number of races which are very proud of that. That was the appeal which Hitler made to the German people, and it is an appeal to *any* race. That is a pride of life. It is that which makes us feel superior to someone else. It is found even in religion today. I meet saints who feel they are super-duper saints. As one man said to me, "I heartily approve of your Bible study program on radio." In fact, he has given financially to our program to help keep it going. He said, "I know a lot of people who listen to it, and they need it," but he very frankly told me, "I don't listen to it." He felt that he didn't need it, that he had arrived, that he was a very mature saint. Of course, it proves that he is a very immature saint when he even talks like that. Satan took the Lord Jesus to the pinnacle of the temple and said, "Cast yourself down. A great many people will witness it, and You will demonstrate to them Your superiority." It was probably at a feast time when many would have seen Him, but the Lord Jesus never performed a miracle in order to demonstrate His superiority.

These are the three appeals that the world makes to you and me today. But when we make our tummy our goal in life, when we attempt to make beauty our goal, or even when we attempt to make that which is religious our goal, it leads to the most distorted view of life that is possible. These things are of the world, and they become deadly. We are told that we are not to love these things because God does not love them—He intends to destroy this world system someday. What is our enemy? The world, the flesh, and the Devil. This is the same temptation which Satan brought to Eve and to the Lord Jesus. He has not changed his tactics. He brings this same temptation to you and to me, and we fall for it.

Now John gives us the reason we are not to love this world—

And the world passeth away, and the lust thereof: but he that doeth the will of God abideth for ever [1 John 2:17].

I have always enjoyed going to England and visiting such places as the Tower of London, Tewkesbury Castle, Warwick Castle, Hampton Court, Windsor Castle, and Canterbury. Many of us have ancestors who came from over there, but those folk were a bloody, cruel, vain, and worldly people. Just recall the way Henry VIII took Hampton Court away from Cardinal Wolsey who was the one who had built it. Poor old Cardinal Wolsey before he died said something like this, "If I had only served my God like I served my king, I wouldn't be here today."

My, how Henry VIII could eat! And when he got tired of a wife—he had several—he just sent her to the Tower to be beheaded. Go and look at all of that today—"the world passeth away." What a story of bloodshed is told at the Tower of London, of the pride of life and of the lust of the flesh. The lust of the eyes also—how beautiful Windsor and Hampton Court are! Even the arrangement of the flowers was made by Sir Christopher Wren, the wonderful architect who also built St. Paul's Cathedral. There is a glory that belongs to all of that, but it has already passed away. England is just a third-rate power in the world today and maybe not even a third-rate power. All of that has passed away and the lust of it. Where is the lust of Henry VIII today? It is in one of those tombs over there. Just think of all the glory which is buried in Westminster—all of that has passed away.

When I look back to when I was a young man, I wish that somehow I could reach back there and reclaim some of those days and some of the strength which I had then. I wish I could use for God what I squandered when I was young. "The world is passing away."

"But he that doeth the will of God abideth for ever." Why don't you work at something which is permanent, something which has stability, something which is going to last for eternity?

Little children, it is the last time: and as ye have heard that antichrist shall come, even now are there many an-

tichrists; whereby we know that it is the last time [1 John 2:18].

The word translated "little children" here is slightly different from the word that is translated in the same way back in verse 12. There it is a term of affection and implies all who are born into God's family, God's little born ones, little *bairns* as the Scottish term is. These little children here indicate the first degree of spiritual experience which we have seen in verses 12–14: the fathers at the top, then the young men, and then the little babies. Here John is talking to the little babies again. The little babies haven't grown up yet. They are passing through this world, and the chances are that they have been tripped up by one of these three things which John has just mentioned.

"It is the last time." We are living in the last day here upon the earth. It has been the last time for a long time. This is the age when God is calling out a people for His name. You can say at any time during this period, "*Now* is the acceptable time. *Today* if you will hear His voice." Why the urgency about salvation? Because, my friend, you might not be here tomorrow. Tomorrow I might no longer be heard preaching on the radio. It just might be that we will not be around, so it is important that I give out the Word, and it is important that you hear the Word.

"As ye have heard that antichrist shall come, even now are there many antichrists; whereby we know that it is the last time." Many antichrists had already appeared in John's day, but there is coming the Antichrist. What do we mean by *antichrist?* I think that this word has been misunderstood and, as a result, the person who is coming has been misunderstood. *Antichrist* is made up of two words: the title *Christ* and the preposition *anti.* It is important to see that *anti* has two meanings. It can mean "against." If I am anti-something, that means I am against that thing. *Anti* can also mean "instead of, an imitation of." Therefore, it can be a substitute. It can be either a very good substitute or just a subterfuge for something.

The question arises, therefore: Is the Antichrist to be a false Christ or is he an enemy of Christ? Where does Scripture place the emphasis? There are several references to Antichrist in 1 John, but the only things we can derive from this verse is that there is going to be the Antichrist and that there were already many antichrists in John's day. What was the thing which identified an antichrist? He was one who denied the deity of Christ. That is the primary definition of an antichrist which we are given in 1 John, as we shall see when we come to verse 22. This is the emphasis in 1 John, but you will recall that the Lord Jesus said, ". . . many shall come in my name, saying, I am Christ; and shall deceive many" (Matt. 24:5). That is antichrist—instead of Christ, claiming to be Christ.

I personally believe that there are going to be two persons at the end of the age who will fulfill both of these types—being against Christ and claiming to be Christ. Scripture presents it that way in Revelation 13. There we have presented a "wild beast" who comes out of the sea, and Satan is the one who calls him forth. That is the political ruler, and he is definitely *against* Christ. There is a second beast who comes out of the land. He appears to be a lamb, but he is a wolf in sheep's clothing. He *pretends to be* Christ who is ". . . the Lamb of God, which taketh away the sin of the world" (John 1:29). He will be a religious ruler. The political ruler will come out of the gentile world, the former Roman Empire. The religious ruler will come out of the nation Israel—they would not accept him as their Messiah unless he did. So that you have actually two persons who will together fulfill this term *antichrist*. They are coming at the end of the age, and both of them can be called Antichrist—one against Christ and the other instead of Christ.

> **They went out from us, but they were not of us; for if they had been of us, they would no doubt have continued with us: but they went out, that they might be made manifest that they were not all of us [1 John 2:19].**

This is very solemn. John says that some who had made a profession of being Christians in that day had all the outward trappings of being Christians. They bore the Christian name, and they identified themselves with some local assembly, some church. They were baptized, immersed, in the name of the Father, the Son, and the Holy Spirit. They took the bread and the cup at the communion service. But John says that the way you can tell whether or not one is really a child of God is that eventually a man will show his true colors and will leave the assembly of God if he is not a child of God. He will withdraw from the Christians, the body of believers, and he will go right back into the world.

We see in 2 Peter what I call "the parable of the prodigal pig." Peter speaks in that epistle of ". . . the sow that was washed . . ." (2 Pet. 2:22). Not only did a son get down in the pigpen, but also a little pig got washed. A little girl pig went up to the Father's house, became very religious, got all cleaned up with a pink bow around her neck and her teeth washed with Pepsodent, but she found she didn't like the Father's house because she was a pig. So one day she said, "I'm going to arise and go to my father, my old man." Her old man was down in a big loblolly of mud. The little pig went home, and when she saw her old man, she squealed, made a leap, and landed in the mud right by the side of him. Why? Because she was a pig. "They went out from us, but they were not of us." That's a harsh, cruel statement, but it happens to be a true statement. There are many who make professions of being Christians, but they are not really Christians.

Remember that the Lord said of Judas, "But, behold, the hand of him that betrayeth me is with me on the table" (Luke 22:21). Right there, at the first communion service, there was a traitor, Judas Iscariot, and he was one who was identified with the group of faithful disciples. We read in John 6:70, "Jesus answered them, Have not I chosen you twelve, and one of you is a demon?" Judas was never anything else although he looked like an apostle, he acted like an apostle, and he had power, I believe, to perform miracles. He went out with the others, and they were not able to identify him as being a phony, but he was.

John makes a very solemn and serious statement here, and he makes this statement to us today. The Lord Jesus said to a very religious man, Nicodemus, that he must be born again. He said to him that night, "Except a man be born again, he cannot see the kingdom of God" (John 3:3). John says here, "They went out from us, but they were not of us." They looked as if they were true children of God, but they actually were not, and the real test, of course, was the Word of God. This ought to cause every Christian, including this poor preacher who writes this, to ask himself the question: Have I really faced up to my sins in the light of the Cross of the Lord Jesus Christ? Have I come to God in repentance, owning my guilt and acknowledging my iniquity? Have I cast myself upon Him and Him only for my salvation? Have I evidence in my life of being a regenerate soul of God? Do I love the Word of God? Do I want the Word of God? Is it bread to me? Is it meat to me? Is it drink to me? Do I love the brethren? And do I love the Lord Jesus Christ? These are the things which we need to consider, my friends, and the Word of God enjoins us in this particular connection.

After presenting justification by faith in no uncertain terms, Paul goes on to make it clear in Galatians 6:15, "For in Christ Jesus neither circumcision availeth any thing, nor uncircumcision, but a new creation." You cannot even boast of the grace of God and say, "Oh, I don't trust in church membership. I don't trust in baptism." Well, whether or not you believe they are necessary for your salvation, the essential question is: Have you really been born again? Or, perhaps you are one who is trusting in these things. Again the important question is: Are you a new creation in Christ Jesus?

Paul spoke to the Corinthians, some of whom had reason to believe they might not be children of God: "Examine yourselves, whether ye be in the faith; prove your own selves. Know ye not your own selves, how that Jesus Christ is in you, except ye be reprobates?" (2 Cor. 13:5). My friend, it is very important that you really know that you are a child of God. Paul also wrote earlier to the believers in Corinth, "Watch ye, stand fast in the faith, quit you like men, be strong" (1 Cor. 16:13). Friend, how are you doing with the Christian life? Are you really a child of God today? Is there evidence in your life that you are a child of God? I'm not talking about whether you have committed a sin or not, but what did you do after you committed the sin? Did you continue on in sin? The Prodigal Son got into a pigpen, but he did not continue there—that was not his permanent address. If you had mailed him a letter after he had been there a few weeks or months, unless the pigs had forwarded it, he wouldn't have gotten your letter. That was no longer his address; he had gone home. The child of God, after he has sinned, is going to go to God with hot tears coursing down his cheeks and crying out to Him in confession. If he doesn't do that, he's not God's child.

God's child must hate sin. This light view of sin which we have today is simply something that is not quite scriptural. I am afraid that there are many church members who are just taking it for granted that they are children of God because they are as active as termites in the church—and they have just about the same effect as termites.

Let me pass this little story on to you. I have heard it told several different ways, and I don't know which way is accurate. Years ago in London, living down in the slums, there was a woman of the underworld, a prostitute. She had a little son, and she became terribly sick. She was frightened because she knew she was dying, and she sent her little son to get a minister, as she put it, "to get me in." She told the little fellow, "You go get a minister to get me in."

The little fellow went out looking for a church. He had to go a long way before he found a very imposing looking church. He went around to the rectory, and the minister came to the door when he rang the bell. The minister looked at this little urchin and said, "What do you want?" The little boy replied, "My old lady is dying. She wants you to come and get her in." At first the minister thought the boy meant that his mother was out drunk somewhere, so he said, "Get a policeman. It's raining tonight, and I don't want to go out. Get a policeman to get her home." The little fellow said, "She's already home. She's not drunk. She is home in bed, and she is dying. She wants somebody to get her in, and she wants me to get a minister. Would you come?" That liberal minister was stunned for a moment. He knew that he should go, that he couldn't turn down a request like that, so he got his coat and umbrella, and he went with the little fellow. They walked and walked and came finally to a very poor section of London and found the creaky stairs which led to an upstairs bedroom.

All the way over, the minister had thought, *What will I say to her? I can't say to her what I have always preached to my people.* He had always told his congregation that they were people of culture and refinement, that they were to keep that up and continue to be very cultured and refined. He thought, *What in the world can I say to her? I can't even tell her to reform. She ought to be reformed, but it is too late now. What can I tell her?* Then he remembered that as a boy his mother had always quoted John 3:16, and in desperation he turned to that verse when he sat down beside this woman. It actually wasn't too familiar to him, but he read it to her: ". . . God so loved the world, that he gave his only begotten Son, that whosoever believeth in him should not perish, but have everlasting life." The dear woman wanted to go over the verse with him. She said, "Do you mean that in spite of the type of person I am, all I have to do is just trust in Jesus?" He said, "Well, that is what it says here. It says that God gave His Son to die on a cross. It says, 'As Moses lifted up the serpent in the wilderness, even so must the Son of man be lifted up' (see John 3:14). That is what I read here, and so that is what you are to do." This dear woman, before she died, right there accepted Christ as her Savior. The preacher himself told the story afterwards, and he said, "That night I not only got her in, but I got *myself* in." My friend, are you sure that *you* are in? Are you sure that you have trusted Him and that He is your Savior?

Some people will write me and say, "You have no right to ask questions like that because we have been members of the church for thirty years." Well, I think you ought to examine yourselves and see whether you are in the faith or not. It is wonderful to make an inventory and find out where you are. There was a time in the Thru the Bible radio ministry when we didn't know where we were financially because our accountant became too ill to help us. When we got an accountant, we found that, although we had thought we were sailing along on nice, blue seas, we really weren't. Thank the Lord, we found it out in time—but it was only because we *examined* our condition. A great many church members need to *examine* themselves. Are you really in the faith? Do you really trust Christ? Someone will say, "You are robbing me of my assurance of salvation." My friend, I believe in the security of believers, but I also believe in the insecurity of make-believers. We need to examine ourselves to see what kind of believer we really are.

At the beginning of this chapter, John made it very clear that we can know that we are God's children and that we can have fellowship with Him. In spite of the fact that we are His feeble, frail, faltering, falling little children, we can still have fellowship with Him because the blood of Jesus Christ, God's Son, just keeps on cleansing us from all sin. We have an Advocate up there with the Father, and He's for us—He is on our side.

Then beginning at verse 3 we saw that God is love. This is the very heart of this epistle. Love is mentioned about thirty-three times. John said that the dear children may have fellowship with each other by walking in love. In other words, the little children must recognize that they are called to live a different kind of life. They now have been given a new nature. They now can live for God. Obedience is the test of life. We can know whether we really have life or not if we keep His commandments—and not only His commandments but His Word. Obeying His Word means we are willing to go even farther than anything he had commanded.

The difference between law and grace is brought out by what John has said. The law said: If a man do, he shall live. But grace says the opposite: If a man live, he will do. That is, a man must have a life from God before he can live for God. He cannot by the old nature live for God. This is the radical difference between law and grace. The law says, "Do," but grace says, "Believe." It is a different approach to the same goal. The only problem is that law never did work for man because it is impossible for the old nature to please God. We all have come short of the glory of God. John showed that the real test is: Do I delight in the will of God? Do I love His commandments? If you are a child of God, you have a new nature, and now you want to please Him. It has been expressed like this in a little jingle:

> My old companions, fare you well.
> I cannot go with you to hell.
>
> I mean with Jesus Christ to dwell.
> I will go with Him, and tell.
>   —Author unknown

That may be a very poor piece of poetry, but it certainly expresses it as it really is. You cannot be having fellowship with God and other believers if you are living in sin.

Proverbs 28:13 says, "He that covereth his sins shall not prosper: but whoso confesseth and forsaketh them shall have mercy." Though we know that the blood of Christ does indeed cover us from all sin, we cannot walk and live in sin and at the same time have fellowship with God and with other believers. If you and I have a life which commends the gospel, it is another assurance that is given to us. I personally do not think you can have real assurance down deep in your heart unless you are obedient unto God. I believe that you can know beyond the peradventure of a doubt that you are a child of God. Such assurance is not presumptuous, it is not audacious, it is not being arrogant, it is not effrontery, it is not a gratuitous assumption, it is not overconfidence, it is not self-deception, it is not wild boasting, it is not self-assertion. In fact, it is true humility. Knowing that you are saved and the eternal security of the believer are not the same; they are not synonymous, although they are related. The Lord Jesus said, "My sheep hear my voice, and I know them, and they follow me: And I give unto them eternal life; and they shall never perish, neither shall any man pluck them out of my hand" (John 10:27–28). If you are His sheep, you will hear His voice. You are not boasting when you say that you know you are saved. You are saying that you have a wonderful Shepherd. You are not saying that you are wonderful but that your Shepherd is wonderful. What a tremendous truth this is!

But ye have an unction from the Holy One, and ye know all things [1 John 2:20].

What John means here by "unction" is anointing. We have an anointing, and that is the anointing of the Holy Spirit. We are going to see this later in verse 27 where John says, "But the anointing which ye have received of him abideth in you."

"But ye have an unction from the Holy One, and ye know all things." The Holy Spirit indwells every real believer and is able to reveal to him all things. ". . . Eye hath not seen, nor ear heard, neither have entered into the heart of man, the things which God hath prepared for them that love him. But God hath revealed them unto us by his Spirit . . ." (1 Cor. 2:9–10) so that we have someone dwelling in us who can reveal to us these things which are in the Word of God. We have an anointing, and every person can have the assurance of his salvation. If you really want to do business with God, if you really want to get right down to the nitty-gritty with Him, come to Him, ask for light, ask for guidance, and ask for His assurance.

"And ye know all things." John means that all the things that you should know as a child of God are potentially yours to know. This does not mean that you have suddenly been given a Ph.D. degree in spiritual things. It does mean that by the Holy Spirit you can study the Word of God, and then through the experiences which God sends to you, you have the possibility of growing in these matters.

Many a child of God grows in grace and in the knowledge of Christ. I have been amazed at the number of lay people whom I have met in my ministry who have done so. The first time I discovered this was when I was a student in my first year in seminary during the depression, way back in the late 1920s. I was asked to go to a little Baptist church in the cotton mill section of Sherman, Texas. I went up there and preached four times that Sunday. I never will forget that! Because the cotton mill hadn't been operating for over a year, they gave me thirty cents for an honorarium! A friend of mine, a fellow student, went with me, and on the way home he asked, "Why are you so quiet?" I told him, "The offering I got was thirty cents!" He said, "Well, this is a real event for you. This is probably the only time that you will ever be paid exactly what you are worth." Thirty cents—but, gracious, that had to be spread over the four sermons which I had given!

We had had dinner, that is, the noon meal, that day in a home where there was an elderly woman whom everybody called "Grandma." (There were about twenty people there, but I don't think she was a grandmother to everybody!) She told me that she had come in a covered wagon in the early days and that she had loaded the rifle for her husband as he had shot at attacking Indians. She had been a real pioneer. But she had never learned to read nor write, and she wasn't able to go to church. The people asked me, "Would you read something to Grandma?" Being a first-year seminary student, I thought I would give her the benefit of my vast knowledge of Scripture (which, by the way, wasn't so vast). I thought I would take something easy and familiar so I began to read John 14. As I went along, I wanted to explain it to Grandma—after all, she couldn't read nor write, and I thought I should help her. I made a comment or two as she sat there, and I thought she looked a little bored. After a few minutes she said, "Young man, had you ever noticed this?" Frankly, she made comments to bring out some things in that passage which I had never heard before. In fact, there was no professor in school who had ever mentioned what she mentioned about that passage of Scripture. Before we got through the chapter, she was telling me and I was listening.

This friend of mine who had come with me was sitting over in the corner, and I knew he was really going to get me for this. On the way home that night, he made another comment. He said, "My, you sure were helpful to Grandma today!" I said, "Where in the world do you suppose that woman learned so much about John 14?" He replied, "Did it ever occur to you that maybe the Holy Spirit is her Teacher? Maybe you and I have been listening to the wrong teachers!" John is saying here that we need to let the Holy Spirit be our Teacher. "Ye have an unction from the Holy One, and ye know all things." That's potential—it is up to you whether you are going to learn or not.

I have not written unto you because ye know not the truth, but because ye know it, and that no lie is of the truth [1 John 2:21].

"I have not written unto you because ye know not the truth"—they had the gospel; they had the truth. John is not writing something new to these folk. He is writing to them for what I think is a twofold purpose. One is to encourage them, and the other is to warn them because there was false teaching going out in that day.

"But because ye know it, and that no lie is of the truth." John is saying that they had the truth, but now lies were coming in. Gnosticism was coming in, and there were many antichrists who were appearing.

Who is an antichrist? We have already said just a few words about this, but now John will say a little bit more—

Who is a liar but he that denieth that Jesus is the Christ?
He is antichrist, that denieth the Father and the Son
[1 John 2:22].

The language is much stronger here; it is, "Who is *the* liar?" In other words, all lies are summed up in the one who is the prince of liars, the Devil. There is coming a man who is Satan's man, and he is *the* liar. And a liar is one who does not tell the truth.

"Who is a liar, but he that denieth that Jesus is the Christ? He is antichrist, that denieth the Father and the Son." John gives us now the definition of antichrist. This will be the embodiment of *the* Antichrist, but there are many antichrists. There were some in John's day; there have been some down to our day, and there are many today. Who are they? They are easy to recognize—they are those who deny the *deity* of the Lord Jesus Christ, those who deny that Jesus the man is the Christ, the Messiah, the one who is God, the one whose name is Wonderful, Counselor, the Mighty God, the one who is pictured in the Old Testament. To deny that is being antichrist.

We have many systems in the world today which deny Him. They are against Christ, and they also imitate Him and try to take His place. In the early church it was Gnosticism. Irenaeus made this statement, "They [that is, the Gnostics] say that Jesus was the son of Joseph and born after the manner of other men." That is the way Irenaeus identified the Gnostics in his day.

Liberalism and all of the cults and "isms" today have also denied His deity. Very candidly, I do not mind saying that the rock opera, "Jesus Christ Superstar," is antichrist. It does not by any means present the Jesus of the Bible who is the Savior of the world. Many years ago Dr. William E. Hocking, who was professor of philosophy at

Harvard University, wrote *Living Religions and a World Faith.* He made this statement, "God is in His world, but Buddha, Jesus, Mohammed are in their little private closets, and we shall thank them, but never return to them." You can see that that is simply a direct, rank denial of the deity of Christ. The one "that denieth the Father and the Son"—that will be the sure mark of the Antichrist, and there are many antichrists even today, of course.

John has identified antichrist for us as the one who denies the Father and the Son. Now he will make it clear in verse 23 that you cannot deny the Son without denying the Father. You see, the deity of Christ is essential to your salvation because if He is not God, the man who died on the Cross over nineteen hundred years ago cannot be your Savior—in fact, He could not even be His own Savior. None of us as human beings can die for the other. It was necessary for God to become a man in order that you and I might have redemption. Therefore, John says—

Whosoever denieth the Son, the same hath not the Father: [but] he that acknowledgeth the Son hath the Father also [1 John 2:23].

When you say that you believe in God and deny the deity of Christ, you really do not believe in God, certainly not the God of the Bible. The God of the Bible is the one who sent His Son into the world to die for our sins. And since the Son is God, He alone is the one who could make a satisfactory sacrifice to God for our sins. Had he been anyone else other than God, He Himself would have been a sinner.

In the great Riverside Church in New York City when Dr. Harry Emerson Fosdick was the pastor, the cover page of a bulletin at that time said, "Whoever you are that worship here, in whatever household of faith you were born, whatever creed you profess, if you come to this sanctuary to seek the God in whom you believe or to rededicate yourself to the God in whom you do believe, you are welcome." It goes on to say a lot about peace and the fatherhood of God, but I'm nauseated reading that far so I will not quote any more of it. It sounds sweet and flowery; it appeals to the natural man, but John's whole point is that we need to beware of this, for this is antichrist. We need to emphasize this very important verse.

Let that therefore abide in you, which ye have heard from the beginning. If that which ye have heard from the beginning shall remain in you, ye also shall continue in the Son, and in the Father [1 John 2:24].

"Let that therefore abide in you, which ye have heard from the beginning." "The beginning" in 1 John goes back to the incarnation of Christ. That "which ye have heard from the beginning," that which you heard concerning His incarnation, that which you heard concerning His life, that which you heard concerning His death and resurrection—in other words, that which they had heard from the beginning when the apostles began to preach the gospel.

"If that which ye have heard from the beginning shall remain in you, ye also shall continue in the Son, and in the Father." I know a man who heard our Bible-teaching radio program more than twenty years ago in San Diego. I'm not going to tell you about his life before then, but when he heard the broadcast, right there and then he accepted Christ as his Savior. God put him at the head of the Christian Servicemen's Center in San Diego, and it is one of the finest in the world. Down through the years, he has been responsible for leading literally thousands of sailor boys and soldier boys to the Lord. I thank God for the testimony of this man's life because John says that if you abide in Him, that is the evidence that you are a child of God.

It is essential, therefore, to have a living faith which rests in the One who came to this earth more than nineteen hundred years ago. In his Gospel John wrote, ". . . the Word was made [became] flesh, and dwelt among us . . ." (John 1:14). How tremendous that is! "No man hath seen God at any time; the only begotten Son, which is in the bosom of the Father, he hath declared him" (John 1:18). He has "declared"—*exēgeomai*, exegeted God. He has led God out to where we can know about Him because God became a man. That is the only way you and I could know about Him. We *can* now know about God. The important thing in this whole section of Scripture is communion with the Father and with the Son. The emphasis here is not so much upon having life in Christ through faith in Him, but the emphasis is upon having communion and enjoying that fellowship with Him which is so essential.

And this is the promise that he hath promised us, even eternal life [1 John 2:25].

The only kind of life that God offers is eternal life. If you lose it tomorrow or next week or next year, it isn't eternal life that you have. It is some other kind of life, but not eternal life.

These things have I written unto you concerning them that seduce you [1 John 2:26].

Seduce means "to lead astray, to lead from the truth." I think that *seduce* is a good word here because it applies in exactly the same way in both the physical and spiritual realms. In other words, you lead a person to commit spiritual adultery when you lead him away from the truth.

Even in John's day there were those coming along who were beginning to deny the Father and the Son, beginning to deny that the Lord Jesus Christ was who He claimed to be. They were seducing some of those who were professing Christians. John says that the thing which you must hold onto is that God has promised you eternal life if you put your faith in Christ, and you do not need to add anything to that.

John was telling the people of his day that they did not need what the Gnostics were teaching. The Gnostics pretended to have super-duper knowledge, that they knew a little bit more than anyone else. I am afraid that in our own day there is a real danger when a great many people are going to so many Bible classes. There is the danger of their becoming super-duper saints. A lady said something to me the other day which I didn't appreciate very much because I know her husband so well and he is a wonderful Christian. She's been going to Bible classes, and they have been fine classes. Don't misunderstand me, I'm not criticizing the Bible classes. However, she was adopting a very superior attitude toward her husband, that she knew more than he knew, and that she was really the one who could teach him. Very frankly, I don't think she could. He is a very intelligent man, and although he is not able to be in as many Bible classes as she is, what he does hear has an effect upon his life. So there is a real danger of present-day Gnosticism, of professing to have a superknowledge and maybe even a super experience, of becoming a super-duper saint where there is just no one else at your level.

Such a position is a dangerous one to come to because if you come into a knowledge of Christ and you begin to grow in grace and knowledge of Him, you will have the same experience that John the Baptist had, which he expressed this way, "He [Christ] must increase, but I must decrease" (John 3:30).

I'm going to make a confession to you, and I hope you won't let it out but will just keep it in the family. In one sense it is a little disturbing to me that my study of the Word of God does not reveal how much I know, but rather it reveals how much I don't know and how woefully ignorant I am. I am studying the Bible now as I never have in my entire life, but when I graduated from seminary, I practically knew it all; there was very little that I thought I needed to learn after that. There were certain things I thought I knew at that time, but very frankly, I'm coming now to find that I didn't know them at all. I thought I did, but I didn't know them at all. There is a vast field of knowledge today for the child of God. It behooves us to make this matter of coming to know Christ through His Word a serious business and to give it top priority in our lives. That is the thing that is all important, and all that John is really saying is, "I don't want you to become a super-duper saint. I want you to rest upon the promise of God."

Now John is going to say to them, "You know Him as your Savior—hold on to that—but now you also want to have communion with Him and the Father, and to have fellowship with Him and the Father and with other believers."

But the anointing which ye have received of him abideth in you, and ye need not that any man teach you: but as the same anointing teacheth you of all things, and is

**truth, and is no lie, and even as it hath taught you, ye
shall abide in him [1 John 2:27].**

"Anointing" is the Greek word *charisma*. We speak of a certain
speaker or preacher as having charisma. If he doesn't have charisma,
he doesn't get very far today, you'll have to admit that. When I went to
my classical dictionary, I must say I was shocked and disappointed.
This word means "to smear on"; it means to take an ointment and
smear it on. It is like when you take a medicated petrolatum and put it
on your chest at night—you are anointing yourself, you are smearing
it on. That is literally what *charisma* means. I checked with Dr. R. C.
Trench and Dr. Marvin Vincent, two outstanding Greek scholars, and
they also have come up with the same meaning. *Charisma* means "to
smear on."

But what does this mean for us today as believers? Back in the Old
Testament, by the command of God, the Israelite priests were anointed
with oil. That anointing indicated in a physical way that they were
specially endued by the Holy Spirit to perform a certain function.
That is what the anointing here means for us today. "But the anointing
which ye have received of him"—that is, you and I have received an
anointing of God. When you are saved, one of the things which the
Spirit of God does for you is that He anoints you. He anoints you to
understand divine truth which you could not understand before.

"But the anointing which ye have received of him abideth in you,
and ye need not that any man teach you." The important thing to note
here is that John is not saying that we do not need teachers. We *do*
need teachers, or else Paul was certainly wrong in Ephesians when he
made the statement that God has given to the church certain men who
are gifted—some who are teachers, some who are evangelists, and
some who are shepherds to minister to and counsel folk. Paul said that
God has given these men to the church to build up the body of believers. I think it is important that we all sit under good teachers.

As I think back over my life, I thank God for the godly men who
have crossed my pathway. They are the ones who are responsible for
my being in the ministry. I have the pictures of four men hanging on
the wall of my office at the headquarters of our radio ministry. The

combined influence of these four men is the reason that I entered the ministry. These men affected my life. You may not know these men, but I am going to give you their names. The first man is a man by the name of Joe Boyd who was a layman in Nashville, Tennessee. When no one else seemed interested in a young fellow who wanted to study for the ministry, Joe Boyd got interested. He is actually the man who did the footwork of making it possible for me to get a job so that I could go to college and for me to get a loan so that I could go to college and seminary. He followed my ministry, and I was his pastor for three years. He was a wonderful man, and I thank God for him. Next to his picture is the picture of the pastor whom I followed in that church in Nashville, Dr. A. S. Allen. He is one of those unsung preachers whom you never hear about today, but he is one of the greatest preachers I ever listened to. Next to his picture is that of Dr. Lewis Sperry Chafer, the founder and first president of Dallas Theological Seminary. My, when I heard him preach, that's what turned me on. I thought, *This is the thing that I want to do.* Next to Dr. Chafer is the picture of probably the brainiest man whom I have ever met, Dr. Albert Dudley. He is a man who had great influence upon the turn which I took in the ministry to become an expository preacher rather than a preacherette giving little sermonettes to Christianettes. I thank God for him and for all these men.

Therefore, John is not saying that teachers are not essential, but he is saying something that is important for God's children today. "But the anointing which ye have received of him"—this has been referred to before when he spoke of "the unction of the Holy One," the anointing of the Holy Spirit. One of the Holy Spirit's ministries is to teach us. He is able to guide us into all truth. The Lord Jesus, the great Teacher, said, "But the Comforter, which is the Holy Ghost, whom the Father will send in my name, he shall teach you all things, and bring all things to your remembrance, whatsoever I have said unto you" (John 14:26). The Holy Spirit will teach us all things, that is, all that you and I are able to contain.

"But as the same anointing teacheth you of all things, and is truth, and is no lie, and even as it hath taught you, ye shall abide in him." There has been given to you an anointing whereby you are *enabled* to understand all truth because ". . . the natural man receiveth not the things of the Spirit of God: for they are foolishness unto him: neither can he know them, because they are spiritually discerned" (1 Cor. 2:14). Paul also wrote earlier, ". . . Eye hath not seen, nor ear heard, neither have entered into the heart of man, the things which God hath prepared for them that love him. But God hath revealed them unto us by his Spirit . . ." (1 Cor. 2:9–10). This is the anointing of the Holy Spirit for a believer.

This is one reason we encourage folk to get into the Word of God and to study it. I received a letter from a dear lady who makes a tape recording of our radio program and then listens to it again and again. She also reads repeatedly the passage of Scripture being taught. All of a sudden her eyes are opened, and she sees the Lord Jesus in a new way. What has happened? She has had an anointing. I don't believe in a lot of the silly stuff that is going on today which is purely emotional and which doesn't enlighten you to understand and love the Word of God and to love the Lord Jesus. It does not matter how much whoopee you put into your religion, you can just whoop it up and have all kinds of emotion, but all that is of no value. It is *enlightenment* that we need today.

The whole point is that there ought to come a day when you and I can stand on our two feet as far as the Word of God is concerned and, as Peter says, ". . . be ready always to give an answer to every man that asketh you a reason of the hope that is in you with meekness and fear" (1 Pet. 3:15). We ought to be able to do that. But there is also a grave danger in this which I want to very carefully point out. I know people who have been going to Bible classes and have been studying the Bible for years, but they never get anywhere. They are the ones who bring Bible teaching into disrepute. I see people at Bible conferences in the summertime—I've seen them there every summer for thirty years—and they are today right where they were thirty years ago. They are like ". . . silly women laden with sins, led away with divers lusts, Ever learning, and never able to come to the knowledge of the truth" (2 Tim. 3:6–7). They don't seem quite to arrive, but they always have their Bibles and are always writing a few little notes down. At a summer conference where I was speaking sometime ago, a woman came to me with the same question that I am confident she had asked me twenty-five years ago at another summer conference! She had a notebook, and she was still taking it down—"ever learning, and never able to come to the knowledge of the truth."

In other words, we ought to get to the place where the Spirit of God is our Teacher. As you study the Word of God, do you ask the Spirit of God to teach you and to lead you? If you don't understand something the first time, get down on your knees and say, "Lord, I miss the point. I don't understand this. Make it real to me. I want this to be real to me." This is important, and this is what John is saying here. "The anointing which ye have received of him abideth in you, and ye need not that any man teach you." There are certain things which the Spirit of God can make very real to you.

"But as the same anointing teacheth you of all things, and is truth, and is no lie." The Lord Jesus said, "For there shall arise false Christs, and false prophets, and shall shew great signs and wonders; insomuch that, if it were possible, they shall deceive the very elect" (Matt. 24:24). But it will not be possible to deceive the elect. The Antichrist will not deceive the elect who are left on the earth when he comes. And today no antichrist will deceive them. I knew a couple who had recently been saved, and they got into a liberal church. I met them when I was a pastor in downtown Los Angeles. They told me, "We worked our way down Wilshire Boulevard, going from church to church until we got to your church. We knew we were not hearing the truth of God at the churches we visited, but we couldn't put our finger on it. We knew the teaching was wrong, but we didn't know *how* it was wrong"—they were just new converts. God's little children are going to follow the pattern the Lord Jesus spoke of when He said, "My sheep hear my voice . . ." (John 10:27). God's children are not going to follow a false shepherd. They hear His voice, and the Spirit of God can be their Teacher. This should be a great comfort to us. We need to test every teacher we hear—it would be well if you tested me. Ask the Holy Spirit, "Is this that McGee is teaching the truth of God? Make it real to my heart, too. I want to know for myself whether it is true or not."

And now, little children, abide in him; that, when he shall appear, we may have confidence, and not be ashamed before him at his coming [1 John 2:28].

"And now, little children"—dear little bairns, little born ones, meaning all God's children, irrespective of maturity.

"Abide in him." This is not really the imperative here but the indicative. In other words, John is saying, "You *are* abiding in Him." I want to repeat that John is speaking here of fellowship. To abide in the Lord Jesus is to live in fellowship with Him. To abide in Him means to have communion with Him.

"That, *when* he shall appear." This is actually, "*If* he appear," but the *if* is not one of doubt. The *if* hasn't anything in the world to do with a doubt of the fact of His coming, but it has to do with the uncertainty as to the circumstances. Although we may have an anointing, we *do not* know when Jesus is coming. That is one thing which He has reserved for Himself to know.

Why has He not revealed to us the time of His coming? "That, when he shall appear, we may have confidence, and not be ashamed before him at his coming." A Christian ought to live in the light of the *imminent* coming of Christ. If you tell me today that He is not coming for another ten years (I may not live that long!), then I do not need to worry about today, and I can be a little careless in my living. But if He might come today, if He came right at this moment, He would catch me preparing this Bible study and that would be fine. I hope He will come at a time like that, but I don't know when He will come. There are times when I get behind a driver who won't let me around to pass him, and I tell him what I think of him. If the Lord were to come at that moment, I might be ashamed at His appearance. So you and I need to be living all the time in the light of His imminent return.

"When he shall appear, we may have confidence, and not be ashamed before him at his coming." A great many people are talking about the coming of Christ, and they get very excited about it; but it certainly is going to be embarrassing for them because they will not have any confidence and they are going to be ashamed before Him at His coming. Why? Because of their lives. The Lord Jesus says, "And, behold, I come quickly; and my reward is with me, to give every man according as his work shall be" (Rev. 22:12). Many people will look around for their reward, and they will find that they haven't got any. Paul wrote, "If any man's work shall be burned, he shall suffer loss: but he himself shall be saved; yet so as by fire" (1 Cor. 3:15). It is very important to have a life that commends the gospel.

John is saying here the same thing that Peter said: False doctrine and false living go together; true doctrine and true living go together. Every now and then you hear of a cult leader who is in trouble because he is guilty either of adultery, or of taking money which doesn't belong to him, or of beating some person out of money. Why? False doctrine leads to false living. True doctrine leads to true living. There is nothing that will affect your life as much as the knowledge that you are going to stand in the presence of Christ and give an account of your works. Every believer will stand before the judgment seat of Christ. Paul writes, "For we must all appear before the judgment seat of Christ; that every one may receive the things done in his body, according to that he hath done, whether it be good or bad" (2 Cor. 5:10). The issue of salvation has already been settled because we are His children and in His presence. It is not a question of whether you are saved or lost; it is a question of whether or not you are going to get any reward or recognition. There will be some folk who will not get any recognition. Paul writes further, "Knowing therefore the terror of the Lord, we persuade men . . ." (2 Cor. 5:11). The Rapture is not going to be such a thrilling event for a great many believers because of the lives they lived down here.

If ye know that he is righteous, ye know that every one that doeth righteousness is born of him [1 John 2:29].

This is the final proof, this is the litmus paper which is put into the solution to tell whether it is acid or base. It surely will tell every time. The Word of God is the real test. In effect John is saying that God's children look like the Father—they take after their Father. If they don't take after the Father, they must not be the Father's children. It is just as simple as that, my friend.

CHAPTER 3

THEME: How the dear children may know each other and live together; the Father's love for his children; the two natures of the believer in action

HOW THE DEAR CHILDREN MAY KNOW EACH OTHER AND LIVE TOGETHER

The last verse of chapter 2 belongs here with the first three verses of chapter 3. First John 2:29 reads: "If ye know that he is righteous, ye know that every one that doeth righteousness is born of him." It is one thing to testify that we know Christ and are in Him; it is quite another to have a life that reveals that He is our righteousness. It is wonderful to know positionally that we are in Christ and that we are accepted in the Beloved, but it is altogether different to have a life down here that is commensurate with that. John is telling us that the way we recognize other believers is by their lives and not by their lips. Righteousness is a family characteristic of the Father and His children. God's children take after their Father—they have *His* characteristics.

THE FATHER'S LOVE FOR HIS CHILDREN

Behold, what manner of love the Father hath bestowed upon us, that we should be called the sons of God: therefore the world knoweth us not, because it knew him not [1 John 3:1].

This is a very wonderful statement that John makes here. Let me give you my very literal translation of this verse: "Behold ye, of what sort of love the Father hath bestowed upon (given to) us, that we should be named children of God, and we are: and because of this the world does not know (begin to understand) us, because it did not know (begin to understand) Him."

John is saying that we do not *expect to be* the sons of God, we *are* the sons of God. A better translation includes the words "*and we are.*" The child of God can say emphatically, "I am a child of God through faith in Jesus Christ." We don't hope to be, we don't expect to be, but the thrilling fact is that every believer can exult and rejoice and constantly thank Him that he is God's child. We are boasters not in ourselves, but we are boasting of the wonderful Shepherd that we have. John makes it perfectly clear that if you are a born again child of God, you are going to exhibit a life that conforms to the Father. A child of God need not be in the false position of saying as an old hymn says:

> 'Tis a point I long to know,
> Oft it causes anxious thought,
> Do I love my Lord or no?
> Am I His, or am I not?
> —Author unknown

John says, "Now we are the children of God"—*right now* we are the children of God.

"Behold, what manner of love the Father hath bestowed upon us, that we should be called the sons of God." The kind of love that John is talking about is a strange kind of love, an unusual kind of love, a kind of love to which we are not accustomed. God loves us. What manner of love the Father has for us! The love of God—that is, His love for us— is shed abroad in our hearts by the Holy Spirit. John will go on to show that God has demonstrated His love by giving His Son to die for us. How many of us have someone who would die for us? How many folk would you be willing to die for? God loves you, and He has proven His love—He gave His Son to die for you.

The greatest motivating force in the world is God's love. Love is the greatest drive in the human family. A man falls in love with a woman, a woman falls in love with a man, and some make such tremendous sacrifices for each other. When human love is genuine love, it is a beautiful thing, it is a noble thing, it is a wonderful thing, and it is a tremendous drive. But God's love for His children far exceeds anything we can experience on the human plane.

The true child of God is going to prove his spiritual birth by being obedient to God's Word. God's wonderful love for us should motivate us. It is that which is going to cause us to want to live for God. Behold, what an unusual kind, what a different kind of love the Father hath bestowed upon us that we should be called the children of God.

John has emphasized that we are God's children *right now.* This brings me to say that our salvation is in three tenses: I have been saved; I am being saved; and I shall be saved.

1. *I have been saved.* The Lord Jesus said, "Verily, verily, I say unto you, He that heareth my word, and believeth on him that sent me, hath everlasting life, and shall not come into condemnation; but is passed from death unto life" (John 5:24). The moment you trust Christ you receive everlasting life, and you will never be any more saved than you are the moment you trust Him. You are born again, born into the family of God. John is addressing "little children"—these are God's children. He says, "What manner of love the Father hath bestowed upon us." Why? Because we are His children. He has bestowed His love upon His children, and they respond to that love by obedience unto Him and by living a life that is well pleasing to Him.

2. *I am being saved.* Paul said, ". . . work out your own salvation with fear and trembling. For it is God which worketh in you both to will and to do of his good pleasure" (Phil. 2:12–13). Peter said, "But grow in grace, and in the knowledge of our Lord and Saviour Jesus Christ . . ." (2 Pet. 3:18). John is talking to us along the same lines here. If we are the children of God, we are going to be obedient unto Him, we are going to grow, we are going to develop, and we are going to go on in the Christian faith. Therefore, we can say that we are being saved.

3. *I will be saved.* When the Lord Jesus comes again for His own, we will experience the final stage of our salvation. Sin no longer will have power over us, and we will be with the Lord forever.

Beloved, now are we the sons of God, and it doth not yet appear what we shall be: but we know that, when he shall appear, we shall be like him; for we shall see him as he is [1 John 3:2].

"Beloved, now are we the sons of God"—not tomorrow, but right now—that is the wonderful part of it. The world won't understand us, that's for sure, because it didn't understand Him. It takes a spiritual insight, and that comes through the anointing which we have talked about that He has given to us. The Spirit of God is the one who can make this real to us, and only the Spirit of God can do that, my friend. Until He confirms it to your heart, of course, you must say, "I don't know whether I am saved." But the Spirit of God can confirm this to your heart.

John says, "Beloved, now are we the sons of God." But someone says to me, "McGee, I'm a little discouraged with you. I think you ought to be a little farther along." I would agree with you on that. I wish I were a better man, and I wish I knew more about the Word of God. Yes, I'd be willing to go along with that—I ought to be farther along than I am. But don't you be discouraged with me, and then I won't be discouraged with you because of the fact that "it doth not yet appear what we shall be."

"But we know that, when he shall appear, we shall be like him." This is a wonderful prospect! He sees in you and in me what He will make out of us. I'm thankful that God is not through with me. If I thought He was through with me now, I would be very much discouraged, but He is yet to perform a work.

The story is told that when a great big piece of marble was brought in to him, Michelangelo walked around it, looking at it, and then said, "My, isn't it beautiful!" One of his helpers who was standing there said, "Well, all I see is a great big piece of marble—that's all." Michelangelo exclaimed, "Oh, I forgot. You don't see what I see. I see a statue of David there." The helper looked again and replied, "Well, I don't see it." Michelangelo said, "That is because it is now in my own mind, but I am going to translate it into this piece of marble." And that is what he did. God says, "It doth not yet appear what you shall be." He sees what He is going to make out of us someday. We are discouraged when we look at each other as we are now, but God sees us as we shall be when He shall appear and we shall be like Him. What a glorious prospect this is for us!

"We shall be like him; for we shall see him as he is." We are going to see the glorified Christ. We are not going to be equal to Him, but we are going to be like Him in our own way. This does not mean that all of us are going to be little robots or simply little duplicates—it is not that at all. We will be like Him but with our own personalities, our own individualities, our own selves. He will never destroy the person of Vernon McGee. He'll not destroy the person that you are, but He is going to bring you up to the full measure, the stature where you will be like Him not identical to Him, but like Him.

It is going to be wonderful in heaven that we will love everybody—I'm excited about that. But the most wonderful thing about heaven to me is that everybody is going to love me! That's going to be quite a change, and I'm looking forward to it. "Beloved, now are we the sons of God, and it doth not yet appear what we shall be: but we know that, when he shall appear, we shall be like him; for we shall see him as he is." This is another great incentive to Christian living. I do not think there is anything else quite like it.

And every man that hath this hope in him purifieth himself, even as he is pure [1 John 3:3].

If you believe that Jesus is coming and that someday you are going to be like Him, that will cause you to live a pure life down here. I know of nothing that is such a great incentive for holy living. We are not wonderful now, but we shall be wonderful someday.

There is nothing that should encourage holy living like the study of Bible prophecy. Today we see a lot of careless, slipshod living, but also a great emphasis on prophecy. I hear people say, "Oh, I'm waiting for the Lord to come!" Brother, my question is not whether you are looking for the Lord to come, but how are you living down here? How you live down here determines whether or not you are really looking for the Lord to come.

We are going to accomplish our goal someday. The New Jerusalem where we will live is going to be a place where He will wipe away all tears. There'll be no sorrow, there'll be no suffering. All of that is wonderful, but the most wonderful thing that strikes me in Revelation 21 is that He says, ". . . Behold, I make all things *new . . .*" (Rev. 21:5, italics mine). That is what I like. I do not know about you, I can speak only for myself, but I very frankly make this confession: I have never really been the man that I've wanted to be. I am at the age now where I guess a man begins to dream a little. And as I look back over my life, I realize I've never been the man that I have wanted to be, and I've never been the preacher I have wanted to be. I've never really preached the sermon that I wanted to preach. People have been kind to me and have said nice things, and I appreciate that, but I know in my own heart that I wish I could do better.

I've never been the husband that I've wanted to be. Previously I mentioned an illness I had several years ago which necessitated a three-month rest. My wife and I sat out on our patio and did a great deal of reminiscing. As I reviewed my life, I thought, *My, I wish I had been a better husband than I was. I should have been.* And I've never been the father that I wanted to be. Some people think I'm a little too much for my grandsons. Well, I'm trying to make up for them what I left out for my own child.

I've never really attained my goal. I thank God for the way He has led me. He's been good to me in my life, and I rejoice in the fact that He's given to me a Bible-teaching radio ministry. I never thought He'd do that, but He has. I have not attained my goal, but He says, "Behold, I make all things new." He is saying, "Vernon McGee"—and He is saying this to you, too—"we are going to be able to start all over again. You are really going to live an eternal life, and you are going to attain your goal." Won't that be wonderful to grow in grace and the knowledge of Him, not only in this life, but for all eternity? What a prospect lies before us!

John is telling us here of the wonderful love the Father has for His children. I have been saved, I am being saved, and I am going to be saved. It's going to be wonderful someday. So you don't be discouraged with me, and I won't be discouraged with you.

THE TWO NATURES OF THE BELIEVER IN ACTION

Whosoever committeth sin transgresseth also the law: for sin is the transgression of the law [1 John 3:4].

Again let me give you my very literal translation of this verse: "Everyone that doeth sin, doeth also lawlessness, and sin is lawlessness." I have before me two very fine Greek commentaries, and they make it clear that the word translated "committeth" sin is literally "doeth" sin, meaning one who lives continually and habitually in sin. You know folk like that. I used to live that way, and the fellows working around me in the bank lived that way. Frankly, working in the bank was secondary. Our interest was in women, in liquor, and in having a good time. That was what we thought life was all about in those days, and that was what we called living. We lived in it continually, and we talked about it continually. That is what John means here: "Whosoever committeth sin"—whoever goes on committing sin, whoever simply *lives* in sin.

"Transgresseth also the law." God *has* made certain laws. God *did* say, "Thou shalt not commit adultery" (Exod. 20:14), and He means that today also. All of this free, new way of looking at things is not a new way at all. It is as old as the hills. The fact of the matter is that it goes back to the jungle, it goes back to paganism.

"For sin is the transgression of the law." God has put up the Law so that we can know that we are sinners, so that we can know what He requires. That is the purpose of the Law. The Law was never given to save, it was given to *reveal* to man that he is a sinner.

Sin is basically and fundamentally that which is contrary to the will of God. In other words, a sinner is one who is insubordinate to the will of God. A little girl was asked in Sunday school to give her definition of what sin is. She said, "I think it is anything that you like to do." You know, she wasn't far from the truth, because this old nature that you and I have is absolutely contrary to the will of God. Paul emphasizes that in Romans 8:5, "For they that are after the flesh [the old nature] do mind [obey] the things of the flesh; but they that are after the Spirit the things of the Spirit." How are you living? In the flesh or in the Spirit?

Paul goes on to say, "For to be carnally minded is death . . ." Death is separation from God, and that is the thing which John is talking about. You cannot have fellowship with Him and be a carnal Christian. It is impossible to do that. I am afraid that there is too much talk today about, "Oh, how I love God, how I am serving Him, and How wonderful He is." How pious some folk are! But, my friend, they are not in fellowship with Him because ". . . to be carnally minded is death; but to be spiritually minded is life and peace. Because the carnal mind is enmity against God [that is, disobedient to God]: for it is not subject to the law of God, neither indeed can be" (Rom. 8:6–7).

Paul makes it clear that before the Law was given there was sin, but it wasn't transgression. The statement here in 1 John, "Whosoever committeth sin transgresseth also the law," does not give a complete definition and is not really a good translation. That is why in my translation I have put it like this: "Everyone that doeth sin, doeth also *lawlessness.*" Paul wrote earlier in Romans, ". . . for where no law is, there is no transgression" (Rom. 4:15); but there is *sin* because he says, "Wherefore, as by one man sin entered into the world, and death by sin; and so death passed upon all men, for that all have sinned" (Rom. 5:12). That is, we sinned in Adam—his sin was ours. "For until the law sin was in the world: but sin is not imputed when there is no law" (Rom. 5:13). Man was still a sinner and was insubordinate to God; nevertheless, it was not transgression of the Law—because the Law hadn't been given yet.

We read further in Romans: "Nevertheless death reigned from Adam to Moses, even over them that had not sinned after the similitude of Adam's transgression, who is the figure of him that was to come" (Rom. 5:14). They sinned—why? Because they were sinners. In Isaiah 53:6 we have a true picture of every unsaved man: "All we like sheep have gone astray; we have turned every one to his own way; and the LORD hath laid on him the iniquity of us all." Everyone has turned to his own way. Those three words tell our story: *his own way.* What's *your* problem? What's *my* problem? We want to have our way. The little baby in the crib is squealing at the top of his voice—what's the matter with the little fellow? He wants his own way! We are born with that nature, a nature which is in rebellion against God.

This is the way the hymn "I Was a Wandering Sheep" by Horatius Bonar puts it:

> I was a wandering sheep,
>> I did not love the fold,
> I did not love my Shepherd's voice,
>> I would not be controlled:
>
> I was a wayward child,
>> I did not love my home,
> I did not love my Father's voice,
>> I loved afar to roam.

But the child of God has now come to God, and he has been born again.

And ye know that he was manifested to take away our sins; and in him is no sin [1 John 3:5].

Only the Lord Jesus can take away sin. He came for that purpose.

Two things are important for us to see here. In John's Gospel he wrote, ". . . Behold the Lamb of God, which taketh away the sin of the world" (John 1:29). He bore the *penalty* of sin. "For God so loved the world, that he gave his only begotten Son, that whosoever believeth in him should not perish, but have everlasting life" (John 3:16). Christ died for the sin of the world. Now here in John's epistle he shows that Christ takes away the *practice* of sin in the life of the believer. Christ is the "propitiation for our sins: and not for ours only, but also for the sins of the whole world" (1 John 2:2). What is the difference? Well, He died a redemptive death to pay the *penalty* of our sin, but He also died that He might deliver us from the *power* of sin right here and now.

"And in him is no sin." The literal translation of this is: "in Him sin is not." He died a redemptive death—He was our sin offering. He was without sin; He was without spot or blemish as was the Levitical sin offering. Therefore He is able to remove the guilt of sin and to provide the power to deliver us from the habit of sinning. He has given to us a new nature that we might live for Him today.

Whosoever abideth in him sinneth not: whosoever sinneth hath not seen him, neither known him [1 John 3:6].

"Whosoever abideth in him sinneth not"—that is, that new nature of yours will not sin; it never sins. Dr. H. A. Ironside puts it this way: "[Christ], this absolutely sinless One, who in grace became sin for us that we might be reconciled to God, dwells by the Spirit in the believer, and our new nature is really His very life imparted to us." If you are God's child, that new nature will not go along with the old nature and commit sin. The believer who abides in Christ does not practice sin—he doesn't live in it. The sinner lives in it all the time, but the child of God has a new nature, and he cannot live a sinful life. This is pictured for us in the story of the Prodigal Son (see Luke 15:11–24). Only pigs live in pigpens; sons do not. Somebody will say, "But the son got into the pigpen." He surely did, my friend, but he got out of the pigpen, too—let's remember that. The child of God can get into it, but he will get out. Why? Because he is a son of the Father, and he takes after his Father. His Father is righteous, and the son wants to live that kind of life.

God provides the power to deliver from the habit of sinning, and that is all that John is saying here—"Whosoever abideth in him sinneth not." Now if you go off to the pigpen, that's the old nature, and if you stay in that pigpen, you never were God's child. If you can be happy in sin, my friend, then you are not God's child because God's children have the nature of their Father. Sometime ago I received a letter from a young man, which may help to illustrate my point here:

> I come to you with a very critical problem and hope that you will help me for I am desperate and have nothing left to try or anybody to turn to. . . . I know that I am a new born again Christian, although many times I had doubts. But I know that I have been saved. Brother, I don't know what you are going to think when you find that I am a homosexual. Perhaps you'd think that I am living in false assurance of eternal life, but, believe me, this is not the case. I know I'm saved, but I lost the joy

of my salvation for awhile. And I try to live a Christian life, and I never was so miserable. . . .

This young man's letter is actually encouraging because he says that he is a homosexual but that he is *miserable* in it. He has no joy; he has no peace. Of course, he doesn't. I will not question whether or not he is a child of God, but I do want to say something to him and to the many others who are just like him: My friend, God can give you deliverance from it. You need to claim that from Him. Ask Him to bring you to the place of peace and joy in your life. If you are God's child, you will never be content in a sinful state. The people are wrong who maintain that homosexuality is merely another life-style. God calls it sin, and God says there is a deliverance. Now there may be an abnormality involved. I am confident that consulting a Christian psychologist would help, but make sure you go to a true Christian psychologist. The other crowd would probably push you farther into your problem, and you would never be delivered out of it. God *can* and *will* deliver you because you are His child. That is what the Word of God says here, and if you believe it, God can deliver you.

Little children, let no man deceive you: he that doeth righteousness is righteous, even as he is righteous [1 John 3:7].

"Little children"—John is talking to those who are God's children; he is not talking to the world.

"Little children, let no man deceive you: he that doeth righteousness is righteous, even as he is righteous." This is the thing which reveals the child of God. To abide in Him does not mean just positionally. It is true that you have a position in Christ that can never be disturbed, but there is also a practical consideration down here. If you abide in Him in fellowship and service, sin must be given up.

I talked to a young man in Phoenix, Arizona, one time who said to me, "Dr. McGee, I've been listening to you on the radio. I think you can help me. I'm an alcoholic. I accepted Christ several years ago, and

I can go for a long time without drinking, but then I will again find myself drunk. I hate myself." This fine looking young fellow who was an executive began to weep as he talked. He said, "I know eventually it will affect my job if I keep this thing up. I don't want to drink, because I am a child of God. And don't tell me I'm not because I have accepted Christ. I've driven fifty miles to get here this morning so that I might ask you this question: Is there deliverance for me?" I told him there was. If he has the nature of his Father, there is one thing that is sure—God will not let him be content and happy in his sin. That was an unhappy young man, the most unhappy young man I had seen in a long time. I told him, "Every time you fall down, brother, go back to your heavenly Father and tell Him what you did. Tell Him that you don't want to disgrace Him again. The day will come when He will deliver you." That has been the story of other men, and it is the story of any sinner who professes Christ and finds himself bound down by a habit. God can and will deliver him.

I happen to be a fellow who knows something about that of which I am speaking here. When I was young, God in a very marvelous way intervened in my life. My mother's side of my family were German, and I want to tell you, they were heavy drinkers—the whole outfit. My father was not an alcoholic, but he was also a heavy drinker. I grew up in that atmosphere, and I started out that way. I thank God for a deliverance from it when I was still just a boy. My friend, I know He can deliver you, and He will deliver you from your sin. This epistle deals with living, right where we are. You cannot simply take some little course and get the deliverance. You are going to have to call upon God for it and have real contact with Him.

> **He that committeth sin is of the devil; for the devil sin-**
> **neth from the beginning. For this purpose the Son of**
> **God was manifested, that he might destroy the works of**
> **the devil [1 John 3:8].**

"He that committeth sin is of the devil." We need to recognize that the Devil is the source of all sin. He is the one who is responsible for sin being brought into the world. He is the one who led our first parents into sin. And the reason that you and I have a sinful nature today is because of the Devil. "He that committeth sin is of the devil." Remember that the Lord Jesus said to the religious rulers of His day, "Ye are of your father the devil, and the lusts of your father ye will do . . ." (John 8:44). The interesting thing is that we will take after our father. If your father is the Devil, then you are going to act like him. If your father is our heavenly Father, then you have His nature, and you are going to act like Him.

"For the devil sinneth from the beginning"—that is, he started out sinning, and he has been at it ever since. He is in rebellion against God.

"For this purpose the Son of God was manifested, that he might destroy the works of the devil." Only Jesus Christ can deliver you, my friend. Go to Him. Don't come to me because I cannot help, and no one else can either. But He can, He is the Great Physician, and I urge you to go to Him with your problem.

The Lord Jesus Christ died for the sin of the world. John the Baptist said, ". . . Behold the Lamb of God, which taketh away the sin of the world" (John 1:29). He took away the penalty of sin. Since you've trusted Christ, your sins are behind you, and you are saved in Him. Your sins will never again be brought up as far as your salvation is concerned because you have trusted Him. But John tells us here that the Lord Jesus not only takes away our sin, but He also was manifested to take away our sins—plural. He was without sin—He had no sin nature. "For such an high priest became us, who is holy, harmless, undefiled, separate from sinners . . ." (Heb. 7:26). But He was a human being, and He died as our sin offering, paying the penalty for our sin. But John also says back in verse 5 of this chapter that He was "manifested to take away our sins." The word our is not in the better manuscripts; it is literally "manifested to take away sins"—that is, to take away the sins of all believers. In other words, He died to make it possible for you and me to live the Christian life.

This brings us right to the subject of this section from verse 4 to verse 24: every believer has two natures. This is what Paul talks about at length in Romans 7. He says there, "For the good that I would [the desire of this new nature that I have] I do not [that is, the old nature which has been in control so long takes over]: but the evil which I would not, that I do" (Rom. 7:19). The new nature desires to do good, but the old nature drags its feet. The old nature will not serve God; it is in rebellion against God. Paul writes further, "Because the carnal mind is enmity against God: for it is not subject to the law of God, neither indeed can be. So then they that are in the flesh cannot please God" (Rom. 8:7–8). You cannot please God until you are born again. "But ye are not in the flesh, but in the Spirit, if so be that the Spirit of God dwell in you"—there is no idea of a condition here, but rather Paul is saying, since "that the Spirit of God dwell in you. Now if any man have not the Spirit of Christ, he is none of his" (Rom. 8:9). Let me be very clear that we are talking about born-again believers. We are not talking about professing Christians; we are not talking about church members; we are not talking about those that have simply been baptized without ever having been saved; we are not talking about those that go through a ritual or belong to some system. We are talking about those that have been born again. The Lord Jesus was manifested "that he might destroy the works of the devil," to make it possible for you and me to live for God.

> **Whosoever is born of God doth not commit sin; for his seed remaineth in him: and he cannot sin, because he is born of God [1 John 3:9].**

"Whosoever is born of God"—this is the new birth we have been talking about. This is what the Lord Jesus spoke of when He said to a religious ruler, "Marvel not that I said unto thee, Ye must be born again" (John 3:7).

"Whosoever is born of God doth not commit sin." A child of God is given a new nature, and that new nature does not and will not commit sin. The reason that the prodigal son could not stay in the pigpen is that he was not a pig. He was a son of the Father, and he longed for the Father's house. If you are a child of God, you will want to be in the Father's house, and you will long for it.

"Whosoever is born of God doth not *commit* sin"—unfortunately, this gives a wrong impression here. The idea is not just one act of sin;

the idea is that he does not *live* in sin. John has said earlier in chapter 2, "If any man [any *Christian* man] sin, we have an advocate with the Father"—the believer will sin. However, John makes it very clear that it is God's will that we live without sin: "My little children, these things write I unto you, that ye sin not" (1 John 2:1). Sin is anything contrary to the will of God, but when sin comes into our lives, John says that we have an advocate with the Father, and "If we confess our sins, he is faithful and just to forgive us our sins, and to cleanse us from all unrighteousness" (1 John 1:9). Again, John is talking to believers, and he is saying that believers will sin. Therefore, when John says, "Whosoever is born of God doth not commit sin," he is saying that that new nature will not continue to *live* in a pigpen—never, under any circumstances will it do that.

"For his seed remaineth in him." If you are a child of God, you have a divine nature.

"And he cannot sin." Why? Because he "is born of God." John is talking about something that is real and genuine. He is not talking about some little profession which you made when you went down to the front of a church and shed a few tears. The question is: Have you been *born of God*? I believe in the security of the believers, but I also believe in the insecurity of make-believers. It is well for us to take an inventory and to look at our lives. We must examine ourselves and see whether we are in the faith or not. Are you really a child of God? Do you long after the things of God? That is the important thing.

Someone might say of this young man who is a homosexual, "He cannot be a child of God." I say that he can be; but if he is a child of God, he is going to give up that sin. A prodigal son ought not to be in a pigpen, and he will not live there. He is going to get out. The day will come when he will say, "I will arise and go to my Father." And his Father is not anywhere near that pigpen—He is as far from it as He possibly can be.

Whosoever is born of God does not *practice* sin. He does not go on in sin. When we received a new nature, we did not lose our old nature—that is the problem. No wonder Paul cried out, "O wretched man that I am! who shall deliver me from the body of this death?" (Rom. 7:24). Only the Spirit of God can deliver you, my friend. If you recognize that you are helpless and hopeless, if some sin binds you down, spoils your life, robs you of your joy, and you are miserable, then may I say to you that He can and He will deliver you—if you *want* to be delivered. If you want to get rid of that sin, if you really want to serve Him, if you mean business with Him, He means business with you. "For his seed remaineth in him: and he cannot sin, because he is born of God."

> **In this the children of God are manifest, and the children of the devil: whosoever doeth not righteousness is not of God, neither he that loveth not his brother [1 John 3:10].**

"In this the children of God are manifest, and the children of the devil." I think we need a little more manifesting today because many of the children of God look like they belong to someone else, or at least they look as if they are orphans. There are two families in the world. The teaching of the universal Fatherhood of God and the universal brotherhood of man I consider to be a damnable heresy. The Bible doesn't teach that God looks upon all people as His children. The Lord Jesus said to the religious rulers, "Ye are of your father the devil . . ." (John 8:44). Someone has said that the reason a Christian ought not to marry a non-Christian is that if you marry in the family of the Devil, you are going to have trouble with your father-in-law! How true that is. There are the children of God and the children of the Devil—there are two families in the world.

John is going to show that there are two things which manifest the child of God. Now God knows our hearts and knows whether or not we have really been born again and are His children. But our neighbor next door doesn't know that. The only way for him to know is for the life of God to be manifested in us. It is not necessarily manifested by lip and language, but it is manifested by our living.

I want to use a very homely illustration which I trust will demonstrate the fact that the believer has two natures. I live on a ranch here in California. Now before I go any further, I must tell you about a lady who asked her neighbor, "Did you know that Dr. McGee owns a *ranch* in California? I'm amazed that a poor preacher can own a ranch!" The neighbor laughed and said, "Why didn't you listen to him carefully? He told you how big his ranch is." So I will tell you that my "ranch" is 72 feet wide and 123 feet deep. In the middle of that ranch is my home. But I do have a lot of fruit trees. I have three orange trees, a tangerine tree, a lemon tree, and a plum tree. I have an apricot tree, a fig tree, and quite a few guava bushes. So that is quite a ranch! I love fruit, and I enjoy getting out in my ranch and looking around. Very seldom, when I am at home, does a day pass without my going all the way around my yard, looking at every tree.

Also, I have four avocado trees which had grown wild out here in this dry land, but grafted into them are several very fine varieties of avocados. You can see where the bud is—it is just about as high as my head on one particular tree.

Below that graft, every now and then a branch will come out from the wild or the old nature of that old avocado, and I have to trim it off. Sometimes I am busy in our conference ministry, and I don't get to tend to things like that. The limb will then come out below the bud, and it will bloom and bear fruit. But it's the poorest fruit you can imagine—it's just no good at all. Above the bud, oh, it bears luscious fruit. My problem is to keep those limbs cut off below the bud so that it will not bear fruit down there. I want it to bear fruit up above where it had a new nature. This avocado tree can bear either kind of fruit—it's just up to me which I want.

My friend, I'm just like that avocado tree. I have two natures. I can be mean and live on a pretty low plane. I have a nature that is that way. All of us have that old nature. We never get rid of it in this life, and we all come short of the glory of God. But above that, in my new nature, is where I can bear the fruit of love, joy, peace, longsuffering, etc. I feel good today, and I have the joy of the Lord in my heart, but tomorrow you may find me down in the dumps. Now I ought not to be there, but that is something that happens, and when it does, I'm living in the old nature.

In Galatians Paul tells the believers to learn to walk in the Spirit. You cannot do it yourself. In Romans 7 Paul discovered two things: there is no good in the old nature, and there is no power in the new nature. You must have help. It does not matter who you are, you cannot live the Christian life yourself. It is only by the Spirit of God working in you that you can produce that good fruit, and He *wants* us to produce fruit.

The Lord Jesus said, "I am the true [genuine] vine, and my Father is the husbandman. Every branch in me that beareth not fruit he taketh away: and every branch that beareth fruit, he purgeth it, that it may bring forth more fruit" (John 15:1–2). He wants us to produce fruit, but He also tells us that He will prune us. When I prune that avocado tree up above the graft, it bears better fruit. God prunes us to get good fruit. Sometimes down there in that old nature, we will also bear fruit. That is called the works of the flesh, and they are not very attractive, they are not anything to brag about.

"In this the children of God are manifest, and the children of the devil." You can tell them apart by their fruit. "Wherefore by their fruits ye shall know them" (Matt. 7:20), the Lord Jesus said. As the late Dr. James McGinley used to say, "I'm not to judge you, but I am a fruit inspector." We ought to be able to find a little fruit on our fellow believers, and in 1 John 3:10 John gives us two clear marks of identification of a true child of God.

"Whosoever doeth not righteousness is not of God." It does not matter who he is or what profession he makes, if a person is not trying to live for God, he is not a child of God. It does not matter how active you are—you may be a deacon in the church, you may be as busy as a termite—but John says that the important mark of identification is: "whosoever doeth not righteousness is not of God." That is a strong statement, but John said it, and the Spirit of God said it through him.

"Neither he that loveth not his brother." Here is the second mark of identification. Do you love other Christians? If you are a child of God, you are going to love other Christians.

The word *love* is going to occur again and again in this epistle. We need to get our understanding of it straight right here at the beginning. There are actually three Greek words that are translated by our one English word *love*. The first Greek word is *eros*, and it is never used in the New Testament. It refers to erotic love, having to do with sex. The Greeks talked a great deal about sex, and they had the god Eros and the goddess Aphrodite, the worship of whom involved sex. Again may I say, the word *eros* is never used in the New Testament. The second word, *phileō*, means "friendship." It means a love of the brethren; it is a brother sort of love. The third word, the highest word, is *agapaō*. That is God's love: "For God so *loved* the world . . ." (John 3:16, italics mine). *Agapaō* is the word John uses here as he tells us that we are to love our brother. We hear a great deal of talk today about love, love, love, and many times it is articulated in the context of sex; but in the Bible, love has no relationship to that whatsoever.

"Neither he that loveth not his brother" means that we are to have a concern for our Christian brother; we are to be helpful to him. It does not mean that you necessarily care for his ways, his conversation, or the things that interest him. It does not mean you have to run up and put your arms around him. It means that you are to be concerned for him. You cannot harbor hatred in your heart against another believer. We will see in the next chapter that this love is not something that is sloppy and slippery by any means. It does not mean that you are to help, that is, to be taken in by every Tom, Dick, and Harry who comes along. We are warned to be very careful indeed and to keep our eyes open, but we are to have a love in our hearts for our brethren in the Lord. This love is to be a concerned love, a love that acts, a love that does something beneficial.

For this is the message that ye heard from the beginning, that we should love one another [1 John 3:11].

John often speaks in this epistle about "the beginning." The beginning he is talking about is the incarnation of Christ.

"For this is the message that ye heard from the beginning, that we should love one another." John is merely reaffirming here what the Lord Jesus had taught: "By this shall all men know that ye are my disciples, if ye have love one to another" (John 13:35). This love is to be the mark of Christ's disciples. John says, "What I am telling you is not new. You have heard this from the beginning. The Lord Jesus taught it to us, and all the apostles have taught this. We have heard from the beginning that we should love one another." Love of other believers is something that is woefully lacking today in many places.

> **Not as Cain, who was of that wicked one, and slew his brother. And wherefore slew he him? Because his own works were evil, and his brother's righteous [1 John 3:12].**

"Not as Cain, who was of that wicked one, and slew his brother." Cain and Abel were blood brothers and were very much alike in many ways. But Cain killed his brother. Why? "Wherefore slew he him? Because his own works were evil, and his brother's righteous." What was Cain's problem? His problem was jealousy or envy—that was Cain's sin.

Jealousy is perhaps not the best word to describe Cain's problem. Jealousy has in it the note of suspicion; for example, a man may be jealous of his wife, meaning that he probably loves her but suspects that she may not be faithful to him. Therefore, I think the better word to use here would be *envy*. Envy and jealousy are given in the dictionary as synonyms, but there is a distinction between them without there really being a difference.

Envy is the thing which characterized Cain. He was envious of his brother, and it led to murder. Envy is that which is in the human heart. As someone has said, "The most destructive force in the world is jealousy and envy."

Let me give you a definition of *envy*: "discontent or uneasiness at the sight of another's excellence or good fortune, accompanied with some degree of hatred and a desire to possess equal advantages." That exactly describes Cain. A definition of *envious* would be: "actuated or directed by or proceeding from envy; jealously pained by the excellence or good fortune of another." This kind of distinction should be noted: a woman is not envious or jealous of a man's courage, and it is also true that a man is not jealous of a woman's beauty; rather, we are envious of that which we would desire to have.

Envy and jealousy among believers in the church hurt the cause of

Christ today probably more than anything else. It is that old secret sin that many believers cover up. How many soloists are jealous of another soloist? How many preachers are jealous of another preacher? A great deal of backbiting that goes on in the church has its root in one thing: jealousy. Boy, that is a mean one! And jealousy is the reason that Cain killed Abel—God had accepted his brother's works and not his own.

Marvel not, my brethren, if the world hate you [1 John 3:13].

John says, "Don't act as if some strange or weird thing has happened to you if the world doesn't accept you, because the world is *not* going to accept you." John makes it very clear all the way through this epistle that he is merely passing along the teachings which the Lord Jesus Christ Himself gave. In John 15:18–19 the Lord Jesus said, "If the world hate you, ye know that it hated me before it hated you. If ye were of the world, the world would love his own: but because ye are not of the world, but I have chosen you out of the world, therefore the world hateth you."

This has always been a problem for many of us in the ministry. I have never really appreciated it when anyone would say, "When you were a pastor in such-and-such a place, you were a popular minister." I'm not sure that I care for that because there is a certain crowd I would deeply regret to be popular with. If I ever was popular with them, I should not have been, and I don't want to be popular with them because the Lord Jesus is not popular with that crowd. I watched a minister on television the other night as he had a marvelous opportunity to witness for Christ. But instead he played up to that unbelieving crowd, and he said some nice, flowery, complimentary things, and he was applauded for it. I wondered if there was not sorrow in heaven because he was in a crowd where Jesus was not popular but he was popular with them.

The child of God needs to recognize that the world will hate him. There is an offense of the Cross, but we should guard against magnifying the offense by making ourselves objectionable and obnoxious.

Many Christians do that, and they are rejected, not because they are Christians, but because they are simply obnoxious—they would be obnoxious whether they were Christians or not. Let's make sure that Christ's rejection and our rejection are for the same reason.

We know that we have passed from death unto life, because we love the brethren. He that loveth not his brother abideth in death [1 John 3:14].

"We know that we have passed from death unto life." You can know whether you are a child of God or not. The idea that we cannot know is a big mistake because the Word of God says that we can know that we have passed from death unto life. How do we know it? "Because we love the brethren." Do you have a love in your heart for the brethren?

One of the greatest experiences that I have had in my ministry is to travel throughout this country, speaking at conferences in many places and meeting many wonderful believers. We have had several rather interesting experiences as we have gone on our way. I recall one time when I was in a city in the East, and I felt very much alone. My wife was not with me at the time, and I felt very, very lonesome. I had gone into a restaurant and had just given my order to the waitress when a man sitting at the next table got up and came over to me. He said, "Dr. McGee, I didn't expect to see you here!" I said, "Well, to whom do I have the pleasure of speaking?" He said, "I have never met you before. To tell the truth, I've never seen you before, but I listen to you on the radio. May I sit down?" So he sat down, and he and I had one of the most wonderful times of fellowship. How did we have it? Well, he was a child of God, and I am a child of God. He hadn't even known that I was to be speaking in that area, but he came with his wife to the meetings after I told him about them. We went out after the service for refreshments, and I probably ought to say that he picked up the tab—which to me was a proof that he was a real brother! It is quite wonderful to be in the ministry today and to meet wonderful Christians all around the country.

Another time I was on a golf course in Florida, and there was a couple ahead of us who were slowing us down. I even yelled at them one time because of it. Finally, when we came right up to where they were playing, the man looked up at me and said, "Dr. McGee, I didn't know you were here playing golf. In fact, I didn't even know you were in this part of the country. Were you the fellow who was trying to hurry us along?" When I admitted that I was, he said, "I'll be very frank with you. I've been to the doctor, and I'm not too well yet so I must play slowly." So I had to apologize to the man for my being very rude and abrupt and trying to get him to hurry. Then we just had a wonderful time of fellowship. Our twosome joined his twosome, and we played along together. We got so involved talking that the foursome behind us yelled at us for not moving along! Again, that was someone I had never seen before, and yet I found him to be my brother, and we enjoyed fellowship together. This is what John is talking about. Do you love the brethren? When you can meet around the person of Christ, when you can talk about Christ with other folk, you have a brother or sister, my friend.

"He that loveth not his brother abideth in death." There are those who do not seem to have any concern for the children of God, but you and I are to have a concern. I always look forward to our Bible conference tours because a lot of the folk will be people whom I have never met before. Yet we will have about two weeks of the most wonderful fellowship that you have ever heard of. Why? Because we love the brethren, and that's a proof of our salvation, friend. There is no greater proof than that as far as your heart is concerned.

Whosoever hateth his brother is a murderer: and ye know that no murderer hath eternal life abiding in him [1 John 3:15].

"Whosoever hateth his brother is a murderer." I didn't say that; John said that, and again he is quoting the Lord Jesus. In Matthew 5:21–22 we read, "Ye have heard that it was said by them of old time, Thou shalt not kill; and whosoever shall kill shall be in danger of the judgment: But I say unto you, That whosoever is angry with his brother without a cause shall be in danger of the judgment: and whosoever shall say to his brother, Raca, shall be in danger of the council: but whosoever shall say, Thou fool, shall be in danger of hell fire." May I say to you, these are strong words. The Lord Jesus said that if you have hatred in your heart toward your brother, it means that you are a murderer. Envy and jealousy lead to hatred, and hatred is murder. How many murderers are there around today? By this standard that God has put before us, there are more murderers out of jail than there are in jail.

I am sure you realize that this passage does not teach that an actual murderer cannot be saved. Christ paid the penalty for *all* sins—even taking the life of another. However, when a man is saved, he will no longer live in hatred.

May I remind you that John's emphasis in this section is the two natures of the believer. When you become a child of God, you do not get rid of your old nature. Rather, you have two natures—an old nature and a new nature. We have seen that the new nature is the only nature that can please God. Man in his natural state is unable to please God; the carnal mind is enmity against God. Therefore, as believers, there are times when we feel like praying, and there are times when we do not feel like praying. There is a hymn ("Come Thou Fount" by Robert Robinson) that says:

> Prone to wander, Lord, I feel it
> Prone to leave the God I love.

Someone read that and said that it didn't express his feelings; so he changed the wording. You will find one version in some songbooks, the other version in other songbooks. The other wording is:

> Prone to worship, Lord, I feel it,
> Prone to serve the God I love.

Which is true of a believer? Is he prone to *wander*, or is he prone to *worship*? I would say that both are true. I have a nature that I've discovered is prone to wander. I have another nature that's prone to worship. God says, "If you are My child, then you will manifest My nature. You will manifest that new nature which I have given to you."

Hereby perceive we the love of God, because he laid down his life for us: and we ought to lay down our lives for the brethren [1 John 3:16].

"Hereby perceive we the love of God." You will note that in your Bible *of God* is in italics which means that those words are not in the better manuscripts or not in the manuscripts at all. They were added for clarification, but I don't think they are necessary. It literally says, "Hereby perceive we the love." This is to be our example—the way God loves. How does God love? "Because he laid down his life for us." This is the standard that is put before us.

"And we ought to lay down our lives for the brethren." Now I don't know about you, but I have not come up to that level in my life. Do you know many people who would put their lives on the line for you? And how many of us would be willing to put our lives on the line for someone else? Today we do not see this spirit manifested as it should be. And yet I was greatly touched when I was ill with cancer the first time because several people wrote to me and said that they would be willing to take my cancerous disease to themselves. They wanted me to be able to finish making the tape recordings for our five-year "Thru the Bible" radio program. I had never known anyone who would be willing to go that far. I recognized, of course, that those folk couldn't do that for me. When one has a disease, that is a case where every man bears his own burden. Although they couldn't take my disease, their willingness to do so was the thing that made such a tremendous impression upon my heart and life.

This is the real proof that God loves us: He gave His Son to die for us. That is the standard—He is our example—and John says therefore that we should be willing to lay down our lives for the brethren. Until you and I have come up to that high level, we are not exhibiting the love that we should have for the brethren.

Now how does this love in action work itself out?—

But whoso hath this world's good, and seeth his brother have need, and shutteth up his bowels of compassion from him, how dwelleth the love of God in him? [1 John 3:17].

John is saying that love is not a sentiment; it is that which expresses itself in action. James also had a great deal to say about this in his epistle. There he wrote, "If a brother or sister be naked, and destitute of daily food, And one of you say unto them, Depart in peace, be ye warmed and filled; notwithstanding ye give them not those things which are needful to the body; what doth it profit?" (James 2:15–16). When a brother in need comes to some folk, they simply say, "I'll pray for you, brother." But the important thing is whether or not our love is manifested in what we are doing. One of the most tragic things in the world will be when many believers come into the presence of Christ, having had this world's goods down here and not having used them for the cause of Christ.

In a family situation you may talk about loving, but love is not made in the parlor or in the bedroom; love is made in the kitchen. A man may leave his home at five o'clock in the morning and explain it by saying, "I'm going to work. I have a wife and two children to feed." You might say to him, "I wouldn't worry about them. You are not going to make a fool of yourself by going out and killing yourself working for them, are you?" He will tell you, "I sure am. I love them, and they are mine." If you went up into the kitchen of his home, you would likely find his wife up early in the morning, having burned her fingers taking the biscuits out of the hot oven. The poor girl is tired and weary in the evening when he gets home, and yet she continues to work and to care for the children. You say to her, "I wouldn't be bothered if I were you," but she says, "This man is my husband, and I love him."

Real love gets into action. We see it in a home where there is love between a man and a woman, but what about love among believers? It ought to get into action; it ought to start doing something one for another. Until it does, my friend, it is the worst kind of hypocrisy. You express your love of the brethren by what you do for them, not by what you say. Our tongue is very good at running way ahead of our feet, but true Christianity, the real article, is a matter of the heart and not of the head or the tongue. John tells us very definitely here that if we are children of God, we will manifest this love.

My little children, let us not love in word, neither in tongue; but in deed and in truth [1 John 3:18].

Self-sacrificing love is required of us as believers. It may not be necessary to give our lives, but certainly it is necessary to give of our substance. Christianity is a love relationship.

And hereby we know that we are of the truth, and shall assure our hearts before him [1 John 3:19].

If our lives manifest these things that John has talked about, we will have an assurance when we come before God in prayer. John has made it very clear that it is possible to be ashamed at the appearing of Christ. A great many folk talk about the coming of Christ, but they don't seem to be *doing* anything. When you and I come into His presence, it is going to be a very awesome experience because He is going to demand some fruit. What have you been doing? He said, "If ye love me, keep my commandments" (John 14:15). One of His commandments is to get the Word of God out, to take it to the ends of the earth. Are you involved in that in any way? Are you involved in anything that reveals that you are a child of God?

When I was a boy living out in the country, how wonderfully love was expressed among those people. Whenever anybody got sick, the neighbors would come in and help. I know that there are all kinds of new methods of doing things, but frankly, I'd sure like to get back to that day when the neighbors did come in to help and to take an interest. Today we expect some bureau of the government to take care of an individual and to take him to the hospital which we think is the best place for him. A great many Christians are not getting involved in the very thing that the Lord is interested in, but, my friend, we are going to have to give an account before Him someday.

"My little children, let us not love in word, neither in tongue; but in deed and in truth. And hereby we know that we are of the truth, and shall assure our hearts before him." If you are a child of God and are using your substance—whether you are rich or poor—to get the

Word of God out, God gives you an assurance in your heart that you are in His will and that you are doing the thing He wants done. Then you have an assurance when you go before Him in prayer, and you will have an assurance when you stand before Him someday. Paul had this assurance when he said, "Henceforth there is laid up for me a crown of righteousness . . ." (2 Tim. 4:8)—Paul knew that; he had that assurance.

For if our heart condemn us, God is greater than our heart, and knoweth all things [1 John 3:20].

The child of God can have an assurance, but suppose we are not doing what we should be doing? Does that mean that we have lost our salvation or that we did not have it to begin with? John says, "For if our heart condemn us, God is greater than our heart, and knoweth all things." We don't lose our salvation. If our hearts condemn us, God is greater than our hearts, greater than our lack of assurance. He is going to hear our prayer. Isn't He a wonderful God? When we fail Him, He won't fail us. You may not have any assurance when you go before Him. A great many Christians come to Him really empty-handed: "I have done nothing for You, Lord. I have done nothing at all, and yet I am coming to You in prayer." God is greater than your heart; He will hear your prayer. He is going to deal with you. He will hear and answer according to His will. "For if our heart condemn us, God is greater than our heart, and knoweth all things." You can depend on Him. Even if you don't have assurance, friend, just keep going to Him.

That young man who was struggling with alcoholism said to me, "I've prayed about this," and I said, "Pray some more." He said, "Well, I just don't feel like I have any assurance at all. I've failed Him so." I told him, "God knows your heart. The way you're talking to me, I believe you're sincere, and I believe you mean business. I know that God is going to give you deliverance from this. Of course you don't have any assurance because you've failed Him. But He is greater than your heart, and He knows you, and He knows you are sincere. He is going to deal with you—you can depend on it."

Beloved, if our heart condemn us not, then have we confidence toward God [1 John 3:21].

If our heart does not condemn us, it gives us a confidence, an assurance in prayer. There was a certain minister who meant a great deal to me when I was a young preacher. I always loved to hear him pray because he prayed with assurance. He did not pray to God willy-nilly, shilly shally, mollycoddle—he went to God with great assurance. I always wanted to be on that man's prayer list. I had a feeling that whenever he began to pray, whatever the Lord was doing, He would say, "Wait a minute. I'm going to listen to My child down there. He's praying, and he knows what he is talking about." I wanted to be on that man's prayer list. I even prayed that he would put me on his prayer list, but I didn't ask him to because I felt that it wouldn't be as effective as if he volunteered it. He knew I was pastor of a church and had a great opportunity, and one day he said to me, "Vernon, I'm praying for you." Oh boy, that was a great day! May I say to you, it is wonderful to have assurance when we pray. "If our heart condemn us not, then have we confidence toward God."

And whatsoever we ask, we receive of him, because we keep his commandments, and do those things that are pleasing in his sight [1 John 3:22].

Love in action gives assurance in prayer. When your life is pleasing to God, you can expect Him to hear and answer your prayer. That is something that is desperately needed today. Remember the early church when persecution first broke out and the apostles were warned to stop preaching the name of Jesus. They went back and reported this to the other Christians, and the group went to God in prayer. They didn't pray that the persecution would stop—they didn't pray anything like that. They began their prayer by saying, "Lord, thou art God" (see Acts 4:24). This is the thing which seems to be absent in most churches today. Folk are not sure that our heavenly Father is God, that He *does* run this universe, and that He *is* in charge. John says, "Whatsoever we ask, we receive of him, because we keep his commandments, and do those things that are pleasing in his sight."

And this is his commandment, That we should believe on the name of his Son Jesus Christ, and love one another, as he gave us commandment [1 John 3:23].

In other words, John says, "Don't say you believe on Him and then not love one another." With one breath you praise the Lord and say you trust the Lord Jesus, but then you say how much you dislike So-and-so. John is not talking about a love in which you just go up and put your arms around someone; he's not talking about a love that you just talk about. His love is not in your lip or your language but in your life. It will be expressed in genuine concern for the individual. You will not be gossiping about him. You will not be hurting him in any way. But you will be concerned about him. This is so desperately needed today. This is the Christian life in a nutshell: "That we should believe on the name of his Son Jesus Christ, and love one another, as he gave us commandment."

And he that keepeth his commandments dwelleth in him, and he in him. And hereby we know that he abideth in us, by the Spirit which he hath given us [1 John 3:24].

The Holy Spirit verifies these things to our hearts if we have not grieved Him. We grieve the Holy Spirit when we do not do His will. Jesus said, "If ye love me, keep my commandments" (John 14:15). If we do not do that, we grieve the Holy Spirit. The Holy Spirit is given to every believer, as Paul makes clear in Romans 8:9, "But ye are not in the flesh, but in the Spirit, if [lit., since] so be that the Spirit of God dwell in you. Now if any man have not the Spirit of Christ, he is none of his." The mark that you are a child of God is that you are indwelt by the Spirit of God, and it is the Holy Spirit who will verify these things and make them real to your heart.

CHAPTER 4

*THEME: Warning against false teachers; God is love—
little children will love each other*

WARNING AGAINST FALSE TEACHERS

We have come to a very difficult section of Scripture here in the fourth chapter of 1 John. One of the reasons is that we are dealing with the spirit world which none of us knows too much about. The second reason is that we are in the Devil's territory. As a pastor I found that whenever I would preach about the Devil, he always managed to cause some interruption in the church service. Generally, he would pinch some baby, or someone would cause some kind of disturbance in the service. It is amazing how he works.

This is a very important passage, but there is a danger of going off the deep end here and becoming rather fanatical. I believe that there is an abnormal preoccupation with the occult on the part of many Christians today which is a most dangerous thing, but we do need to know what the Bible teaches about it.

In the first six verses of this chapter, John gives a warning against false teachers, false prophets. He gives us this warning, having just established the fact that we have been given the Spirit of God and that we have been given an anointing to understand the things of God.

Beloved, believe not every spirit, but try the spirits whether they are of God: because many false prophets are gone out into the world [1 John 4:1].

We are dealing here with the spirit world, and the Bible has a great deal to say about it. For instance, we read in Psalm 104:4, "Who maketh his angels spirits; his ministers a flaming fire." That is quoted in Hebrews 1:7, "And of the angels he saith, Who maketh his angels spirits, and his ministers a flame of fire." Down a little farther in the first chapter of Hebrews, we read, "Are they not all ministering spirits, sent forth to minister for them who shall be heirs of salvation?" (Heb. 1:14). I have never seen an angel, and I have never had a visit from one of them. I personally do not feel that they have a ministry to the church today. My belief is that since we are indwelt by the Holy Spirit, no improvement can be made on that arrangement. I would much rather have the uncreated Holy Spirit than a created angel following me around and ministering to me. I think that we need to put the emphasis upon the ministry of the Holy Spirit in our hearts and in our lives.

Not only are there good angels who serve God, but there are also fallen angels. They too are called spirits in the Scriptures. The Gospels speak a great deal of the fact that in Christ's day there were "unclean spirits." That is what is known as demonism; we call them demons because the Scriptures use that term.

As believers we are warned to put on the whole armor of God because we are in a gigantic battle which is beyond the flesh, a battle that is a spiritual battle. Paul writes in Ephesians 6:12, "For we wrestle not against flesh and blood, but against principalities, against powers, against the rulers of the darkness of this world, against spiritual wickedness in high places." As this verse suggests, the Devil had his demons pretty well organized. In his army of demons he has the generals at the top, the lieutenant colonels, and then on down to the sergeants, the corporals, and the plain, ordinary infantrymen or soldiers. I think that God has His angels organized in pretty much the same way.

"Beloved, believe not every spirit, but try [prove] the spirits whether they are of God." A few years ago that sounded rather spooky, but we have moved from the time when the supernatural was ridiculed, especially among the intelligentsia, to a day when Satan has become an obvious reality and is now worshiped openly. Much of this is taking place on or near our college campuses. I know of a couple of satanic churches here in Los Angeles, and there may be many more. What a few years ago was considered to be way out in left field today exists out in the open. The report came from Florida that a young boy of only seventeen years of age was murdered, and they found that it was done to appease Satan. The satanic priestess down there, just a young woman of twenty-two, had said that this boy should be killed!

Quite a few things which have happened in our day are really spooky. We had, for instance, the appearance of the book, *Jonathan Livingston Seagull*. The author, Richard Bach, said that a voice dictated the book to him and that it was not his own style of writing. I understand that many churches recommended the reading of this book and that several good men were taken in by it. It is the story about a theological concept of a young sea gull which has human attributes. He soared off toward unlimited perfection and found that each of us is just an idea of the Great Gull. This book teaches that birth and sin and sickness and death are not realities but only illusions, that what the biblical writers call sins really are virtues, and that freedom is freedom to do what one pleases. All of that is not new but is actually out of the very pit of hell itself—it is satanic.

We are seeing a manifestation of demonism today, and it is all around us. It is strange that this has happened in this materialistic age that once would have nothing in the world to do with the supernatural. When I was in college any concept of the supernatural was frowned upon and looked down upon. It did not make any difference what IQ you had or what grades you made in school, if you believed in the supernatural, you were considerably less than intelligent and you were radically wrong—and they didn't hesitate to tell you so. Today that has all changed. Many young people have gone off the deep end into this because they never have had any Bible training at all.

John has been speaking here to God's children. He has told us how we are to love each other and to help each other, but we must be careful. Paul wrote to the Philippians whom he loved a great deal, "And this I pray, that your love may abound yet more and more in knowledge and in all judgment" (Phil. 1:9). It is a wonderful thing to love, but you and I are in a big, mean, wicked world, and this world we live in will take us in; it will deceive us. We need to be careful. This lovey-dovey idea the liberals have—love slopping over on every side—is not what the Word of God teaches. Paul prayed that the Philippians' love might abound in *knowledge* and *judgment*. Don't be taken in by everyone who comes along and says that he is a Christian, because many of them are not.

When I was first a pastor in downtown Los Angeles, I had to discover through experience that all of the bums—and that's the best word I know for them—will take advantage of you. One Sunday morning after the service, those who had come forward in response to the invitation were being dealt with, when one of them said that he wanted only me to talk to him. I was quite flattered when the personal worker came and said, "This man wants *you* to talk with him." So I went over to him and gave him the plan of salvation. He seemed very interested. In fact, when I would read a verse, he would then take the Bible and read it for himself. (He knew what he should do!) Then he said that he wanted to accept Christ; so we got down on our knees; he shed tears and professed to receive Christ. When we got up, I made the mistake of asking him how he was getting along. He said, "I hate to say this, but my suitcase is down yonder in a hotel." It was one of the cheap hotels in the downtown area. "They won't let me have my suitcase because I can't pay my bill. I'm greatly embarrassed by it." He told me that his bill was seven dollars. Well, what are you going to do for a man who has apparently just accepted the Lord and has lost his suitcase? I gave him seven dollars. I went out and got into our car where my wife was waiting for me. I became very expansive as I told her what I had done and how wonderful it was.

Time went by, and about six weeks later I saw the man's picture in the newspaper. He had been arrested. He said, "I've been living in Los Angeles for six months, and I've lived off the preachers. They are the biggest saps in the world." Well, I happened to have been one of them! I called up a good friend of mine, the late Dr. Bob Shuler, who was then pastor of Trinity Methodist Church. I asked him, "Did he come to see you?" He said "Yes." "Well, did he get to you?" I asked, and he said that he hadn't. When I told Dr. Shuler that he *had* gotten to me, he said, "Well, Vernon, I have been in downtown Los Angeles longer than you have, and I've had a little more experience. Don't let them take you in. Remember that the Bible says to *try* the spirits to see whether they are of God or not. A lot of these men are phonies." Yes, the bum was a phony, and he had taken me for seven dollars, but I had learned my lesson. Paul prayed that the Philippians might not only grow in their love, but in judgment and knowledge. You need to use love wisely. You need to be very careful.

John says here, "Believe not every spirit, but try the spirits." When I hear of some person who seems to have supernatural power, to heal, or to impart a gift, I don't get excited. Someone asks me, "Why don't you go hear So-and-so?" Well, I don't want to waste my time. I am told to test, to prove the spirits. There is a lot of hocus-pocus going on today which I can assure you has nothing supernatural in it at all. It is just camouflaged Christianity.

"Because many false prophets are gone out into the world." The "false prophets" are false *teachers*. Paul used the word that way in 1 Corinthians 14:3, "But he that prophesieth speaketh unto men to edification, and exhortation, and comfort." *Prophesy* here means "to teach, to exhort, to instruct."

There are many teachers abroad today of whom we need to beware. Right now prophecy is becoming an interesting subject and rightly so. But again, the thing which needs to be said was said very well by Sir Robert Anderson: "Beware of the wild utterances of prophecy-mongers." There are many today who are saying more than the Scriptures say so that we need to be very careful. Just because a man comes along saying, "Lord, Lord," does not mean that we should love him. That may be the man who is more dangerous than a rattlesnake because he may be teaching a false doctrine. He may not be really teaching the Word of God, although he carries a big Bible under his arm.

Hearby know ye the Spirit of God: Every spirit that confesseth that Jesus Christ is come in the flesh is of God [1 John 4:2].

"Hearby know ye the Spirit of God." How are we to distinguish? John tells us the way: "Every spirit that confesseth that Jesus Christ is come in the flesh is of God." This is where it all begins—in Bethlehem. Jesus Christ was born in Bethlehem, and it begins there with his incarnation. Calvary and the Garden Tomb are meaningless unless He is who He claimed to be, unless He is the God-man. The way that you can determine the false teachers is that they will deny the deity of the Lord Jesus Christ. That does not mean they do not talk nicely about Him. They talk about what a remarkable youth He was and that He was a superior child who was born into the world. They say that he was a religious genius and that he was intoxicated with God. They say that He probably had a greater knowledge of God than any other man. He was a "superstar," you know. They can say a lot of nice things about Him, but ask them if He was *God manifested in the flesh?*

John speaks of "the Word" in his Gospel. Who was the Word? He was God, and He created all things, and He became flesh. Where? Yonder at Bethlehem, at the Incarnation. Jesus came there. When you deny the Incarnation, the deity of Christ, then you deny His work upon the Cross because it all rests upon who He is. The false teachers attempt to tear Him down by complimenting Him. That is the way the Lord Jesus is being treated today in many circles. But He is who He claimed to be—God of very God.

John is meeting head-on the early heresy of Gnosticism, one of the branches of which said that Christ came upon Jesus at His baptism and left Him at Calvary. That is not what the Word of God teaches. The Word of God says that that Babe in Bethlehem was more than a re-markable baby, that His death upon the Cross was not an ordinary death, and that when He rose from the dead, He rose bodily from the dead. He ". . . was delivered for our offences, and was raised again for our justification" (Rom. 4:25). Isaiah wrote, "For unto us a child is born, unto us a son is given . . ." (Isa. 9:6). The child is *born,* but the Son is *given.* The Son came out of eternity, the Ancient of Days, but the child, His humanity, was conceived in the virgin's womb. He came forth yonder in Bethlehem where a few shepherds and wise men came to worship Him. He was more than just a precocious child. He was the precious Prince of Peace who made peace by the blood of His Cross and some day shall bring peace to this war-weary world that we are living in. The important thing for us to note is that this is the mark of whether a man is a false prophet or not—"*Hereby* know ye the Spirit of God." Let's find out what a person believes about Jesus Christ. That's important, very important.

> **And every spirit that confesseth not that Jesus Christ is come in the flesh is not of God: and this is that spirit of antichrist, whereof ye have heard that it should come; and even now already is it in the world [1 John 4:3].**

This is the third time John has mentioned Antichrist. John is the only writer who mentions him and he does so only in his epistles. In the second chapter of this epistle, John says, "Little children, it is the last time: and as ye have heard that antichrist shall come, even now are there many antichrists; whereby we know that it is the last time" (1 John 2:18). And then again we read, "Who is a liar but he that denieth that Jesus is the Christ? He is antichrist, that denieth the Father and the Son" (1 John 2:22).

As we saw in chapter 2, *anti* can mean two different things. It can mean either "against" or "instead of," that is, an imitation. We have that idea presented in Scripture. The Lord Jesus said, "For many shall come in my name, saying, I am Christ; and shall deceive many" (Matt. 24:5)—in other words, they imitate Him. Antichrist is used, therefore, in the sense of pretending to be Christ. The other meaning is to be against Christ.

Revelation 13 presents to us the two beasts of the end time. The first beast is the great political ruler who is coming—Antichrist to rule the world, a world dictator. Then there is a religious ruler who is coming, and he is called the false prophet. He will cause the world to worship the first beast. He will come like a lamb, but underneath he is a wolf—he will imitate Christ. I believe that there will be two men and that it will take both of them to fulfill all that is said in Scripture about Antichrist. There will be a great *political* ruler at the end of time, and there will be a great *religious* ruler at the end of time.

All our contemporary civilization is building up to the coming of Antichrist. There is coming a great religious ruler, and all the religions of the world will amalgamate under his leadership. The movement is in that direction even today. We also have that same kind of movement politically. There is a moving today toward one ruler for this world. He will bring peace into the world temporarily, but it is going to be the most frightful time the world has ever seen.

In chapter 2 John says, "Even now are there many antichrists" (1 John 2:18), and there are quite a few of them about in our day, but they are not *the* Antichrist. They are false teachers who are moving the world closer and closer to that day, preparing the world for the one finally to appear.

In these first six verses of chapter 4, we have what some have called a parenthesis. Maybe they are not quite that, but this is certainly a red light that John puts up here, a caution sign, a stop-look-and-listen sign. He says that love must be exercised with judgment and knowledge. We are to love believers, but we need to be sure that the so-called believers are not false teachers. We are to prove the spirits, for there are false prophets around who are teaching false things. In John's own day there were the Docetic and Cerinthian Gnostics who denied the humanity of Christ, and in so doing, they also denied the deity of Christ; they made Him out to be a very strange and weird individual.

For some reason, God's people have always been credulous and gullible. There are many believers who fall victim to what Dr. A. T. Robertson called "the latest fads and spiritualistic humbuggery." There is a lot of that going around in our day. Therefore, John spends the time to give us this warning to beware that false teachers will deny the incarnation of Christ. Don't tell me that the virgin birth is not important. Some people ask, "Can you be a Christian and deny the virgin birth?" You cannot—that is impossible because the mark of a false teacher is at that very point. When you destroy the virgin birth, you destroy His death upon the Cross for the sins of the world and His bodily resurrection—in other words, you wreck the Christian faith. This is the reason that the virgin birth is the place where there has been so much denial in our day, and that denial, of course, is that which reveals a false teacher immediately.

John is saying that God's children ought not to be deceived by false teachers. The objective way to identify them is that they deny the incarnation of Christ. Now John gives us the internal, the subjective evidence in verse 4—

Ye are of God, little children, and have overcome them: because greater is he that is in you, than he that is in the world [1 John 4:4].

There is no reason for you to be taken in by satanic teaching or the denial of the deity of Christ. A man said to me once, "I used to be in a certain church, and I was a high officer in the church. Then I got saved, and my eyes were opened. I knew then I was in the wrong place because they were denying the deity of Christ. So I got out." Why did he get out? Well, he was indwelt by the Spirit of God who had revealed the truth to him. "Greater is he that is in you, than he that is in the world"—so that there is no excuse for you to be taken in today by a false teacher, a false prophet, or a false teaching. The thing to do is to go to God and ask that the Holy Spirit lead you and teach you. If you are in fellowship with Him, the Spirit of God is going to make the issue clear to you.

I knew a dear lady right here in Southern California who told me that when she first began to listen to my radio broadcasts, she was very critical of them. She was in a cult, and she felt that what I said contradicted what she was being taught—it sure did! But she began to test it by the Word of God. She was really a born-again Christian but had gotten caught up in this cult. Her eyes were opened because the Spirit of God was there to teach her. "Greater is he that is in you, than he that is in the world." You can overcome all the false teaching you hear because of the indwelling Spirit of God.

Every Christian is indwelt by the Spirit of God. Listen to what Paul has to say: "But ye are not in the flesh, but in the Spirit, if so be that the Spirit of God dwell in you. Now if any man have not the Spirit of Christ, he is *none of his*" (Rom. 8:9, italics mine). Back in the fifth chapter of Romans, Paul tells us of one of the present results of being justified by faith: ". . . the love of God is shed abroad in our hearts by the Holy Ghost which is given unto us" (Rom. 5:5). Again, we read in 1 Corinthians 6:19, "What? know ye not that your body is the temple of the Holy Ghost which is in you, which ye have of God, and ye are not your own?" Was Paul talking to some super-duper saints, some who had really arrived, some very spiritually-minded saints who were living on a high plane? No. He was writing to the Corinthians, and he called them carnal and babes in Christ. The Corinthian Christians were just about everything they should not have been, and yet they were indwelt by the Holy Spirit. Every child of God is indwelt by the Spirit of God.

This is the reason that you do not need an angel to appear to you tonight to tell you what you need to know. Rather, you need to have the Holy Spirit teach you, and the Holy Spirit teaches through His Word. You cannot stay away from the Bible, be ignorant of it, ignore it, and yet expect to have the Spirit of God lead you and guide you. I try to get people into the Word of God because I have seen that the Spirit of God opens people's hearts, and He protects them from this world in which we live. We are living in a big, bad world, and we need to be warned concerning the false teaching that is around us.

John tells us that we can test the teachings of men. This test is just like putting litmus paper into a solution to tell whether it is an acid or a base. This is a test which will work: Does the teaching deny the incarnation of Christ? That is the spirit of antichrist, my friend. You do not want to follow that. It is contrary to Christ, although it may imitate Him. Generally, these false teachers are very attractive persons. Many of them have charisma, and they make a fleshly appeal to folk. But they can be tested by the Word of God for the Holy Spirit is there to be our teacher and guide.

They are of the world: therefore speak they of the world, and the world heareth them [1 John 4:5].

False teachers do get a following. The occult and the cults are growing much faster today than is Christianity. They have the advantage of appealing to the flesh which we do not. I think it is tragic to have Christians using fleshly means to draw in a crowd. We need to be very careful of the methods which we use. If they are fleshly methods, God cannot bless them at all. We need to be sure that the Word of God is being given out. I do not care whether several thousand people come to your church—that is not the important thing. I am interested in the message. Is the Word of God being given out? Is it given out in the power of the Spirit so that the Spirit of God can take it and use it? The message should not be a great deal of pious promotion for some sentimental appeal that causes you to give. The question is: Is the Word of God going out from your church? Are folk coming to know Christ? You would not want to invest money in a company simply because they have a nice, beautiful building and the president is a very handsome fellow with a warm personality and charisma. If you are going to invest in that company, you will want to know whether it is making money or not. Is it getting results? Is something happening there? God intends us to use a little consecrated common sense when we are dealing in the area of religion.

"They are of the world: therefore speak they of the world, and the world heareth them." When John used Cain and Abel as an illustration in chapter 3, he said that Cain was not righteous and was not God's child. He did not say that Cain wasn't *religious*. Cain did bring an offering; in fact, I have a notion his offering was much more attractive than Abel's offering. Cain's was beautiful; it was the fruit of the field, but Abel's was bloody and would have been sickening, nauseating to some people. However, Abel's offering is the one which God accepted because it recognized the sin of man and his need of a Savior. Cain did not recognize that at all. The flesh depends on itself; it does not depend upon God.

John has made very clear to us that the important thing is that Jesus Christ is who he claimed to be, and that is the thing that we need to be very clear on in order to determine whether a teaching is true or not.

We are of God: he that knoweth God heareth us; he that is not of God heareth not us. Hereby know we the spirit of truth, and the spirit of error [1 John 4:6].

I used to tell the people of my church that I use the Bible as a Geiger counter. A Geiger counter tells you whether or not there is uranium there in the rocks and in the soil. So I just run the Geiger counter over the congregation, and the Bible is what I use—it's my Geiger counter. I want to tell you, God's children will always respond to it. That was my confidence as a pastor, and that is my confidence as I write this book: God's people are going to hear. And, my friend, I do not expect the other crowd to hear. If they don't want to hear it, all they have to do is close this book. The Christian ministry does not depend upon them for support; God's people are to support God's work. After all, the ark of the covenant was carried on the shoulders of the priests of Israel. The ark speaks of Christ, and if we are to take Him to the world, we must carry Him on our shoulders. The supreme encouragement of the ministry is to know that God's children will hear you. The elect cannot permanently be deceived. Christ said it is not possible to deceive the elect.

John was sure of who the Lord Jesus was. He could say, "And the Word was made [became] flesh, and dwelt [pitched His tent] among us, (and we beheld his glory, the glory as of the only begotten of the Father,) full of grace and truth" (John 1:14). Then John gave us the purpose of his Gospel: "And many other signs truly did Jesus in the presence of his disciples, which are not written in this book: But these are written, that ye might believe that Jesus is the Christ, the Son of God; and that believing ye might have life through his name" (John 20:30–31). John had indubitable, indestructible, inevitable evidence that Jesus was who He claimed to be. John knew that, and that is something we need to be a little more sure of today.

GOD IS LOVE: LITTLE CHILDREN WILL LOVE EACH OTHER

Beloved, let us love one another: for love is of God; and every one that loveth is born of God, and knoweth God [1 John 4:7].

"Beloved, let us love one another." Why? "For love is of God." Let's be very careful here as to what John is talking about. He has just given a warning against false teachers who are not to be loved—let's be clear on that. I don't pray for them. I do not give any pious platitude, saying, "Oh, I'll pray for them." I'm not praying for them. They are the children of the Devil. I'm praying for God's people, and I'm praying for the lost sinner who will turn to Christ if I can just get the Word to him. Having given a warning against these false teachers, John returns now to the theme of this section: believers are to love one another.

Again, may I say that the word for love here is not *eros*; John is not talking about sex. All through this section, the word for love is *agape* love. It is not sentimental, it is not sexual, and it is not social love. It is supernatural love. It is that which the Holy Spirit can put in our hearts, and only the Spirit of God can make it real to us. It is the love of God, and only the Spirit of God can enable us to extend this love to others.

This is not the kind of love you have for friends whom you delight in being with. I am afraid this verse has been misused by many. When I was a student in college, I used the verse in courting a girl: "Beloved, let us love one another: for love is of God." But the kind of love I was talking about was not the kind John was talking about, I can assure you of that! I surely did misinterpret this, and I must confess that I did not have a very lofty purpose at that particular time. "Beloved, let us love one another"—that is, love other believers.

"Every one that loveth is born of God, and knoweth God." This is approaching it from the human viewpoint. When you meet a person who says he is a believer, and you find that he loves you and loves other brethren, you can know that he is a born-again child of God. I think people write things in letters to me that they probably would not say to me in person. Many people write, "Dr. McGee, I love you," and then they go on to tell me why. One family, for instance, wrote, "You brought our two children to the Lord." Their love for me is an evidence that they are real born-again children of God.

He that loveth not knoweth not God; for God is love [1 John 4:8].

"He that loveth not knoweth not God." This is another test of whether or not you are a child of God. I'm not asking you if you love your papa and your mama. I'm not asking you whether you love your wife or your husband or your children or your kissin' cousins—I'm not asking you that. But I am asking you this: Do you love other believers?

Maybe someone will say, "Well, I can love *some* of them." That is helpful—you are moving in the right direction. There are some believers who are very unlovely, but I think that we can love them in the sense that we can have a concern for them. I do not think it is essential to put your arms around them. The way you can show your love is by your concern for others which is going to result in helping them.

John gives us now another definition of God: "God is love." We have three great definitions of God in this wonderful little book: (1) "God is light" (1 John 1:5), and that was the theme from chapters 1:1 to 2:2; (2) "God is love" (1 John 4:8–16), the very heart of this epistle is the theme from chapters 2:3 to 4:21; and (3) "God is life" is the theme of chapter 5. These are the three great definitions of God which John gives to us, and they constitute the major divisions of this very marvelous epistle.

John says here and again in verse 16, "God is love." Dr. Harry Ironside has a very remarkable story relative to this which I am going to pass on to you because I think it demonstrates in a wonderful way the truth that only Christianity reveals the God of love. In *The Epistles of John* Dr. H. A. Ironside writes:

> Years ago a lady who prided herself on belonging to the intelligentsia said to me, "I have no use for the Bible, for Christian superstition, and religious dogma. It is enough for me to know that God is love." "Well," I said, "do you know it?" "Why, of course I do," she said, "everybody knows that." "Do they know it yonder in India?" I asked. "That poor mother in her distress throwing her little babe into the holy Ganges to be eaten by filthy and repulsive crocodiles as a sacrifice for her sins—does she know that God is love?" "Oh, well, she is ignorant and superstitious," she replied. "Those poor wretched negroes in the jungles of Africa, bowing down to gods of wood and stone, and in constant fear of their fetishes, the poor heathen in other countries, do they know that God is love?" "Perhaps not," she said, "but in a civilized land we all know it." "But how is it that we know it? Who told us so? Where did we

find it out?" "I do not understand what you mean," she said, "for I've always known it." "Let me tell you this," I answered; "no one in the world ever knew it until it was revealed from heaven and recorded in the Word of God. It is here and nowhere else. It is not found in all the literature of the ancients."

In this was manifested the love of God toward us, because that God sent his only begotten Son into the world, that we might live through him [1 John 4:9].

How does God love you? Well, you won't find that love in nature, but you *will* find a bloody tooth and a sharp claw—that is what nature reveals to us. You will find the love of God at Calvary. There is where you find the love of God manifested. "In this was manifested the love of God toward us, because that God sent his only begotten Son into the world, that we might live through him." God has proven His love. He laid down His life for us, and that is the proof of His love. Paul wrote, "For scarcely for a righteous man will one die: yet peradventure for a good man some would even dare to die" (Rom. 5:7). I don't know whether or not you could get anyone to lay down his life for you; I think I'd have a little problem finding someone myself. But God has proven His love by giving His Son to die for you! He gave Him to die for you, not after you won a Sunday school attendance bar for not missing a Sunday in five years, but God loved you when you were yet a *sinner*. "For when we were yet without strength [while we were lost, while we were absolutely unlovely], in due time Christ died for the ungodly" (Rom. 5:6). God loved us! "But God commendeth his love toward us, in that, while we were yet sinners, Christ died for us" (Rom. 5:8). The explanation of this love is found in Him and not in us—because we are not lovely, and some of us do not ever seem to become very lovely.

"God sent his only begotten Son into the world." Here is another verse to which those who would like to rob us of the deity of Christ turn. When Jesus Christ is called "the only begotten Son," it means that He has a unique relationship with the Father. He was not created. God called the created angels His *sons*, and He says that those who trust Christ are *sons* of God, but yet He says that the Lord Jesus is "the only begotten Son." It is interesting that the same thing is said of Isaac: "By faith Abraham, when he was tried, offered up Isaac; and he that had received the promises offered up *his only begotten son*" (Heb. 11:17, italics mine). At that time Abraham already had his son Ishmael, and later on he had other sons. Ishmael was Abraham's son, just as much his son as Isaac was. In fact, Ishmael probably looked as much like Abraham as Isaac ever did. But Isaac is called "his only begotten." Why? Because he was unique, his birth was miraculous, and he stood in a unique relationship which was not shared by Abraham's other sons. The position of the Lord Jesus Christ in the Godhead is that of the eternal Son of the eternal Father. We cannot have an eternal Father without an eternal Son. God is not a father in the sense that a human being is a father. "God is a Spirit" (see John 4:24), the Lord Jesus said. The "only begotten Son" is the Father's unique son. Others are sons by creation, as Adam and the angels, or by new birth, as believers are, but Jesus Christ alone is the unique Son.

"That we might live through him." How are we going to live through Him? We are going to live through Him because He died. His death gives us life.

Herein is love, not that we loved God, but that he loved us, and sent his Son to be the propitiation for our sins [1 John 4:10].

John has used the word *propitiation* previously: "And he is the propitiation for our sins: and not for ours only, but also for the sins of the whole world" (1 John 2:2). This word is quite remarkable. I recognize that there are two different Greek words translated as "propitiation" in the New Testament; actually, it is the same word, but two different forms of it. Dr. A. T. Robertson, whom I consider to be the greatest Greek scholar of them all, writes that here the word *propitiation* is a predicate accusative in apposition with *huion*, that is, the Son.

Propitiation means "mercy seat"; it is the same as the Old Testament word *atonement*, meaning "to cover." Let me make this as clear as I possibly can. In the tabernacle in the Holy of Holies there was the ark of the covenant. On top of that ark there was a highly ornamented lid crowned with two cherubim of solid gold, facing each other and looking down upon the lid of the box. The ark was a very beautiful thing, for it was all made of acacia wood, and covered inside and outside with gold. The lid was called the mercy seat. It was here that the nation of Israel met God in the person of the high priest. Once a year and only once a year, the high priest came into the Holy of Holies, bringing blood to be sprinkled on the mercy seat. That is what made it a mercy seat because they could meet God only in that way. God loved them, but He didn't simply slop over with love and say, "You can come to Me any way you want." This was the way they were to come to God: On that great Day of Atonement, the high priest went in and sprinkled the blood on the mercy seat. That meant that the nation was accepted by God for another year, and then they would need to go through it again the next year.

Now here in the verse before us, the Lord Jesus Christ is called "the propitiation for our sins" which means that He is the mercy seat for our sins. Jesus is Himself the mercy seat because He died down here for us—"Who was delivered for our offences, and was raised again for our justification" (Rom. 4:25). He has made expiation for our sins so that you and I can come with boldness to God's throne of grace. That throne is now a throne of grace because there is mercy there for us. That is what Christ did, and that is the way God demonstrated His love for us.

Twice in this chapter John gives us the definition, "God is love"— in verse 8 and again in verse 16. This is a very wonderful thing, but I would have you notice something about it. You cannot say God is mercy. You cannot say God is grace. You cannot even say God is justice. You can say God is holy because that is what "God is light" means. But you can also say God is love. However, I must add that God does not save us by love. He loves us, and we don't want to lose sight of that, but God just *cannot* open the back door of heaven and slip us in under cover of darkness because He loves us. And God cannot let down the bars of heaven and bring us in the front door. God cannot do that, and God will not do that because He is a holy and righteous God.

We have seen so many shenanigans go on in the execution of justice in this nation of ours, and as a result, the judges and others who are in authority have wanted to get rid of capital punishment. Why? Because they know that if a man has money or influence, his life will not be taken. It is the poor fellow who cannot escape his due punishment. The tragic thing today is that we believe that justice can be bought. My friend, even though God loves you, He does not save you by love, and He *cannot* save you by love. God had to do something about the fact of sin because He is holy and righteous, and what He does is right. So God gave His Son to die on the Cross for you and me, to pay the penalty for our sin so that a holy God can now reach down and save us. It is only on that basis that a holy God can save us. Christ is the mercy seat, and that is where God reveals His love. "For God so loved the world, that he gave his only begotten Son, that whosoever believeth in him should not perish, but have everlasting life" (John 3:16).

"Herein is love, not that we loved God"—we didn't love Him first. God didn't give His Son for us because we were attractive, or because we were good, or because we promised to do something. God loved us "while we were yet sinners." We need to recognize that you and I today are sinners and that ". . . God commendeth his love toward us, in that, while we were yet sinners, Christ died for us" (Rom. 5:8). God did it at that time, and God loved us at that time. He has made a way for us, if we will accept it. Jesus said, ". . . I am the way, the truth, and the life: no man cometh unto the Father, but by me" (John 14:6). You either come His way, or you don't come, my friend. It is nonsense to think that because God is love, everything will work out all right and everyone will ultimately go to heaven. It *is* going to work out all right because the lost are going to a lost eternity, and the saved are going to a saved eternity—that's the reason things are going to work out all right. Are they going to work out all right for you? They will, if you come God's way—this is tremendously important.

Beloved, if God so loved us, we ought also to love one another [1 John 4:11].

God has demonstrated His love for us; therefore, you and I ought to love on that plane. John says, "Beloved, if God *so* loved us." This carries our minds back to verse 10: "Herein is love . . . that he loved us, and sent His Son." He loved us enough to give His Son as a propitiation for our sins.

If we love those who love us, or if there is a selfish motive in our loving them, there is no value in that. The Lord Jesus said, "For if ye love them which love you, what reward have ye? do not even the publicans the same?" (Matt. 5:46).

"We ought also to love one another." I like that—when John says *ought*, he means it. He is not talking about the cheap sentiment which a great many people entertain today. Jesus said, "If ye love me, keep my commandments" (John 14:15). If you really love Him, keep His commandments. "This is my commandment, That ye love one another, as I have loved you" (John 15:12). How about it, my friend? Do you mean to tell me that you can hate Christians down here and still love God? I want to say to you very frankly that if you cannot demonstrate in your life that you have love for other believers, there is a serious question whether you are a child of God or not. There is a lot of nonsense going on today. We are not talking about backslapping, calling somebody "brother," or behaving so nicely in the church. But do you have a concern for believers? Do you have a concern to get out His Word? Do you have a concern to serve Him?

The Lord Jesus could say even on the Cross, ". . . Father, forgive them; for they know not what they do . . ." (Luke 23:34). The first martyr of the church, Stephen, said the same thing. Can you forgive like that today? Are you able to forgive those who have hurt you and harmed you and yet profess to be children of God? And if they cannot return your love, there is some question whether they are children of God or not. This is the real test, the acid test, and it hurts—does it not? We do not hear this type of teaching in these little seminars which talk about how to live the Christian life and how to get along with your spouse. John gives us the bedrock of it all: Do you love God? And do you love other believers?

> **No man hath seen God at any time. If we love one another, God dwelleth in us, and his love is perfected in us [1 John 4:12].**

"No man hath seen God at any time." Some folk challenge this statement by pointing out scriptural illustration of those who have seen God. Of course, there was Adam, and then Moses who talked with God face to face and was hidden in the cleft of the rock as He went by. And Isaiah says, "In the year that king Uzziah died I saw also the Lord sitting upon a throne, high and lifted up, and his train filled the temple" (Isa. 6:1). We find that Ezekiel had visions of God, and the Lord appeared to Daniel and to others. And yet John said in his Gospel, "No man hath seen God at any time." But John does not conclude his statement with that; he goes on to say, ". . . the only begotten Son, which is in the bosom of the Father, he hath declared him" (John 1:18)—that is, He has *exegeted* Him. When God appeared to men in the Old Testament, they did not see God, for God is a Spirit and that is the way we worship Him. Those men saw what is known as a *theophany*. That is, God manifested Himself in some form to these men, but He did not reveal Himself in all of His fullness. So that John says in his epistle, even after the Lord Jesus had gone back to heaven, "No man hath seen God at any time." The Lord Jesus said to Philip, ". . . he that hath seen me hath seen the Father . . ." (John 14:9). But how did they see Him? He was veiled in human flesh, so much so that multitudes who saw Him did not recognize Him. He grew to manhood yonder in Nazareth, veiled in human flesh—they did not know that He was the Son of God. No man has seen God in all of His fullness. That is still true today.

The point that John is making here is that no man has seen God at any time, but God today can manifest Himself through believers loving each other. Since the world in general is not seeing Jesus as He is presented in the Word of God, the only way it will know of God's love is through the lives of believers who represent Him. None of us knew about God's love until God showed it to us on the Cross when Christ died, and He makes it real to us by the Holy Spirit. "And . . . the love of God is shed abroad in our hearts by the Holy Ghost which is given unto us" (Rom. 5:5). And ". . . God commendeth his love toward us, in that, while we were yet sinners [while we were dead in trespasses, while we were ungodly], Christ died for us" (Rom. 5:8). It is still true that there is none that seeketh after God, so God has come down seeking man. He came down nineteen hundred years ago, manifesting Himself in the Lord Jesus Christ, and all I know about God is what I know in the person of Christ. I do not know how God feels about certain things; I do not know what He thinks about certain things. But when I follow the Lord Jesus and listen to Him, I know what God is thinking, I can feel the heartbeat of God. I know how He feels at a funeral, for the Scriptures tells us that "Jesus wept" (John 11:35). I know how He feels about little children because He took them up in His arms and blessed them. I know these things because the Lord came and manifested God.

How is this wicked world in which you and I live to know God? Unfortunately, too many believers are trying to *please* the world instead of trying to *preach* to the world. We are concerned about what the world thinks of us, but the important thing is: What do they think of Jesus? What do they think of us as we represent Him? Someone has put it like this: "At the age of twenty, we do not care what the world thinks of us. At thirty we worry about what the world is thinking of us. At forty we discover that it wasn't thinking of us at all!" That is about true. We today are to witness to the world. How are we going to witness? By giving out the Word? Yes, that is all important. But the world is hungry for love; they do not know what love is. Their definition of love would be a three-letter word spelled s-e-x. That is the love the world knows about, but they don't know anything about the love of God. They do not know how wonderful He is, but He can be manifested in us.

"And his love is perfected in us." His love is developed in us. It is a growth in us. The world is not seeing enough of this love, and yet it has seen it in the lives of a great many believers.

Hereby know we that we dwell in him, and he in us, because he hath given us of his Spirit [1 John 4:13].

You see, it is only by the Holy Spirit within us. This is not a human love. You and I cannot work it up. "But the fruit of the Spirit is love, joy, peace, longsuffering, gentleness, goodness, faith, meekness, temperance: against such there is no law" (Gal. 5:22–23). Love heads the list. Many believe that love is the fruit and that the others stem from love. If you read 1 Corinthians 13, you will come to the conclusion that joy comes out of love and peace comes out of love. In *The Epistles of John* Dr. Ironside records this incident concerning Chiang Kai-shek at the time he was ruling mainland China.

We all noticed a short time ago the account of the professed conversion of the President of China. We hope there has been a real work in his soul, but time will tell. I was reading how he came to his Christian wife who was saved long before he made a profession, and said, "I can't understand these Christians; why, they have been treated most abominably here, they have been robbed, beaten, many of them killed, they have been per-secuted fearfully, and yet I never find one of them retaliating, and any time they can do anything for China, for our people, they are ready to do it; I do not understand them." "Well," said his wife, "that, you see, is the very essence of Christianity. They do that because they are Christians."

There is a need for a great many more pagans to be able to see this love in the lives of believers. This is a teaching that is surely neglected today. How often do you hear this taught in the church, on radio, or in these little seminars which are held? Is this the teaching which is given as being basic and all important?

When the love of God is in a home you don't need to worry about the wife's place and whether she is to obey her husband or whether the husband is to be the head of the house, and all of that argument. Paul writes, "Husbands, love your wives, even as Christ also loved the church, and gave himself for it" (Eph. 5:25). If he loves her, if she is a woman for whom he would lay down his life, if the wife can say that she loves him with all her heart and would do anything for him, then I don't think you need a lot of little rules to go by. There is a monument which I have seen, a statue of a pioneer woman, a fine looking young woman with a sunbonnet on. She has about five children around her holding on to those long skirts which they wore back in those days.

She's holding a gun, and out ahead of her is her husband. She is loading one gun, while he shoots another. He is out there protecting her. Do you know, friend, I don't think that woman needed any lectures on sex. If she had five children, I think she could have given you some lectures on it! And I don't think she needed to have a lecture on how to keep her husband. She had no trouble keeping him. They loved each other, and they were bound together. How wonderful love is! If the child of God could only manifest the love of God to others round about him!

"Hereby know we that we dwell in him, and he in us, because he hath given us of his Spirit." Back in verse 4 John says, "Greater is he that is in you, than he that is in the world." You are indwelt by the Spirit of God, and the Spirit of God *can* produce this love in your heart. You cannot produce it; I cannot produce it. I cannot love like this. My natural bent is that when somebody hits me, I hit back. But if we are filled by the Spirit of God who indwells us, we are going to manifest this kind of love to the world.

And we have seen and do testify that the Father sent the Son to be the Saviour of the world [1 John 4:14].

This is the gospel witness. This is the message which we have to give. This is the purpose of our love. Again I must come back and repeat: Christian love is not sloppy or sentimental; it is not sexual; it is not social. It is not something that you have at the church banquet. It is something which reveals itself when we take Christ to a lost world of sinners. That is the way we manifest our love.

This kind of love is hard to understand. I have been with missionaries in many places—in Israel, in Africa, in Lebanon, in Turkey. I have been with them in France and Italy, and I have been with them in Mexico, in Venezuela, and in the Caribbean. The thing which I have noted about these missionaries is that they love people, and a lot of people they love are very hard to love. But they have a love for them, and it is wonderful to see it. What are they doing? They are taking the gospel out to these people, and that is the thing that God has commanded them to do. When they first got there, maybe they didn't love the people. But after you have ministered to people, my friend, you will love them, or you just couldn't be God's child.

Whosoever shall confess that Jesus is the Son of God, God dwelleth in him, and he in God [1 John 4:15].

This is where you begin with Him—don't tell me that the virgin birth is not important. This is the gospel: ". . . how that Christ died for our sins according to the scriptures; And that he was buried, and that he rose again the third day according to the scriptures" (1 Cor. 15:3–4). My friend, if He is not who He said He was, His death and resurrection are absolutely meaningless; in fact, He was not raised from the dead if He is not who He said He was. But the evidence is all on the side that He did arise from the dead, and the proof of it is that He was virgin born; He was who He claimed to be.

"Jesus is the Son of God, God dwelleth in him, and he in God." This is the reason that the Lord Jesus could say, "Whatever God does, I do." He made this tremendous claim: "Verily, verily, I say unto you, He that heareth my word, and believeth on him that sent me, hath everlasting life, and shall not come into condemnation; but is passed from death unto life" (John 5:24). How is that possible? He had just said in John 5:19, ". . . The Son can do nothing of himself, but what he seeth the Father do: for what things soever he doeth, these also doeth the Son likewise." He is going to raise the dead, and He is going to judge all of the dead. Therefore, He can say to you today that because of who He is, if you will hear His voice and if you will believe on Him, you will be saved.

And we have known and believed the love that God hath to us. God is love; and he that dwelleth in love dwelleth in God, and God in him [1 John 4:16].

These are inextricably intertwined and interwoven together. You simply cannot say that you love God and that you are a child of God when you hate the brethren down here.

This is the second time in this chapter that we have had the definition, "God is love." An easy way to remember where in chapter 4 it occurs is this: multiply four by two and you get eight—it occurs in verse 8 the first time; then multiply eight by two and get sixteen—it occurs in verse 16 the second time. First John 4:8 and 16 give the definition, "God is love."

> **Herein is our love made perfect, that we may have boldness in the day of judgment: because as he is, so are we in this world [1 John 4:17].**

Our love is made "perfect," and that means *complete*.

"That we may have boldness in the day of judgment." If you and I love God, love the Lord Jesus, and love one another as brothers and sisters in the faith, then that will give us boldness, and we will not have any fear of the day of judgment.

"Because as he is, so are we in this world." In other words, we are just like the Lord Jesus. He was raised from the dead, we are told here, and He has life. Well, we have that life too, and He is up yonder at God's right hand for us. We are in Christ, and we are accepted in the Beloved.

Therefore, John can go on to say—

> **There is no fear in love; but perfect love casteth out fear: because fear hath torment. He that feareth is not made perfect in love [1 John 4:18].**

There is nothing like fear in the human heart, but the child of God does not need to fear any judgment which is coming. It was all settled when Christ died for you.

"He that feareth is not made perfect in love." If you are fearful, you cannot enjoy your salvation. Joy stems from love, and if you have love for the Lord Jesus, for God, and for your brethren, then fear has been cast out.

> **We love him, because he first loved us [1 John 4:19].**

He loved us when we were unlovely. He is worth loving. He is worthy. The Lamb is worthy of all of our love, all of our devotion, all of our service.

> **If a man say, I love God, and hateth his brother, he is a liar: for he that loveth not his brother whom he hath seen, how can he love God whom he hath not seen? [1 John 4:20].**

I didn't say this; John said it. John says that if you say you love God and hate your brother, you are a liar.

"For he that loveth not his brother whom he hath seen, how can he love God whom he hath not seen?" There is a great deal of nonsense and pious hypocrisy going on today even in our fundamental churches. If we do not love our brother, then we do not love God either.

> **And this commandment have we from him, That he who loveth God love his brother also [1 John 4:21].**

This is a commandment. God does not ask you if you feel like it or if you want to. He says, "This is what I command you. Because I love, you are to love." I get a little weary hearing the talk of "dedicated" and "consecrated" Christians who are lazy on the job. You are not dedicated to the Lord unless you demonstrate it in your life and in your service.

CHAPTER 5

THEME: God is life; victory over the world; assurance of salvation

GOD IS LIFE

In this chapter we have come to the last major division of this very wonderful little book. In the first part of this epistle, we saw that God is light. In the very extensive center section, we saw that God is love. The subject of this final chapter is God is life.

VICTORY OVER THE WORLD

In these first five verses, John talks about victory for the believer over the world. The "world" here is the *cosmos*, that is, the world with all of its organizations, all of its governments, all of its selfishness, its greed, its sorrow, its sickness, and its awful sin. John is going to say that it is possible for the child of God to have a victory right down here over this world.

Whosoever believeth that Jesus is the Christ is born of God: and every one that loveth him that begat loveth him also that is begotten of him [1 John 5:1].

God is life, and that life comes through being born of God. "Whosoever believeth that Jesus is the Christ is born of God"—this is the method, this is how one is born again. John makes it very clear here and in the opening of his Gospel that you become a child of God through simple faith in the Lord Jesus Christ. "But as many as received him, to them gave he power [the *exousian* power, the right, the authority] to become the sons of God, even to them that [don't do any more nor less than simply] believe on his name" (John 1:12). This means that when you trust Christ, you trust who He is as well as what He did. What He did has no value if He is not who He said He was.

Again I must say that the virgin birth is very essential. Who is this that died for the sins of the world? It was not an ordinary man who did that because an ordinary man is sinful himself and could not even die to obtain his own salvation. He could die only a judgment death, being eternally separated from God. "Whosoever believeth that Jesus is the Christ is born of God." It is faith which produces the New Birth.

Once you have been born again, how do you know that you have been born again? Do you have some great, overwhelming experience? Do you enter some ecstatic state? Not necessarily; some people do I am told, but that is not the usual procedure. "Whosoever believeth that Jesus is the Christ is born of God: and every one that loveth him that begat loveth him also that is begotten of him." When you trust the Lord Jesus Christ, you are born again, and God becomes your heavenly Father. He is God the Father, and He becomes your heavenly Father. If He is your heavenly Father and you are begotten of Him, then you will love Him. But it doesn't stop there—you are also going to love the one who is begotten of Him. In other words, you are going to love other of God's little children. John has said this before, and he has said that it is not something new with him. In 1 John 3:11 we read, "For this is the message that ye heard from the beginning, that we should love one another." And the Lord Jesus said, "By this shall all men know that ye are my disciples, if you have love one to another" (John 13:35).

This expression, "born of God," is very, very important. Being born of God hasn't anything to do with the fact that you have joined a church or gone through a ceremony. If you are born of God, I hope you have joined a church and that you take part in the ordinances of your church, but following certain rituals does not make you a child of God. The important thing is: Are you born of God? Have you been born again? You are born again when you trust the Lord Jesus Christ as your Savior, and the proof of it is that you love God. You love your Father—He begot you—and you are going to love His other children because they are your brothers and sisters. This cannot be confined to a certain denomination, church, race, clique, or group. The one who is born again will love others who are born again.

This is the epistle on how you can have the assurance of your salvation, and all along John has been giving to you some of the evidences that you are a child of God.

1. "If ye know that he is righteous, ye know that every one that doeth righteousness is born of him" (1 John 2:29). A child of God will *practice righteousness* in his life. This does not mean that righteousness is the unusual thing, the abnormal thing, or that once in awhile you practice it. It is to be the practice of your life. You will slip and fall sometimes, but righteousness will be the practice of your life if you are His child.

2. "Whosoever is born of God doth not commit sin; for his seed remaineth in him: and he cannot sin, because he is born of God" (1 John 3:9). A child of God will *not practice sin*. He will not live in it, revel in it, or make it his life. The life-style of a sinner is sin; he lives in sin all the time, and you don't expect him to do differently. We all lived in sin until we came to Christ.

3. "Beloved, let us love one another: for love is of God; and every one that loveth is born of God, and knoweth God" (1 John 4:7). A child of God will *love other Christians*. This is another test that will give assurance to you that you are born of God: Do you love other Christians?

4. "For whatsoever is born of God overcometh the world: and this is the victory that overcometh the world, even our faith" (v. 4). A child of God will *overcome the world*.

5. "We know that whosoever is born of God sinneth not; but he that is begotten of God keepeth himself, and that wicked one toucheth him not" (v. 18). A child of God *keeps himself from Satan*.

Two of the evidences, two of the birthmarks of a child of God are given right here in this chapter. We will discuss these last two in more detail as we come to them. John is going to emphasize certain tests of true sonship—love, obedience, and truth. No one can quarrel with these words. Love, obedience, and truth are marks of the child of God.

By this we know that we love the children of God, when
we love God, and keep his commandments [1 John 5:2].

What does John mean here by "his commandments"? The commandments, as I understand it here, are not referring to the Old Testament law at all, but they are the commandments which the Lord Jesus gave when He was here. For example, we find not ten commandments but about twenty-two in the fifth chapter of 1 Thessalonians: "Rejoice evermore" (v. 16); "Pray without ceasing" (v. 17); and "Quench not the Spirit" (v. 19), etc. These are the commandments for believers today. Every child of God wants to keep these commandments as the practice of his life. This is something that he desires to do, something that he longs to do.

For this is the love of God, that we keep his commandments: and his commandments are not grievous [1 John 5:3].

The New Scofield Reference Bible has changed "grievous" to *burdensome.* I'm not going to quarrel with that because it is a good translation, but the literal is really, *heavy.* His commandments are not heavy. This does not mean that they are difficult to keep but rather that they do not impose a burden when they are kept. John is saying that the child of God *wants* to keep His commandments. It is something that he wants to practice; it is not difficult for him to do these things at all. The little girl who was carrying a big, heavy baby was asked by a concerned woman, "Little girl, isn't that baby too heavy for you?" The child replied, "He's not heavy. He's my brother." It makes all the difference in the world, you see, when he's your brother. "For this is the love of God, that we keep his commandments: and his commandments are not grievous." The point is that they impose no burden on us because we are keeping them through love.

The story is told about a man and his family who years ago drove into a little town in Oklahoma in a covered wagon. They stopped at the town store to talk to the owner as he sat on an apple box out in front of the store. "What kind of town is this here?" they asked him. The storekeeper said, "Well, what kind of town did you come from?" "Oh," the man said, "we came from a wonderful town. Everybody there seemed to know each other, and had a concern for each other.

They were very wonderful people. We really hated to leave, but we wanted to move west. We're not sure where to settle down. What kind of town is this?" The storekeeper said, "This is just the same kind of town which you left. It's that kind of town." The man said, "Well, then, I think maybe we'll settle here," and they drove on down the street.

In a little while another covered wagon drove up in front of the little store. The man asked the storekeeper, "What kind of town is this?" So the storekeeper again said, "What kind of town did you leave?" "We were glad to get away from it," the man said. "They were some of the meanest people that I have ever met. They were never very neighborly or very helpful. We never had any friends there, and that's the reason we left." The storekeeper told him. "Well, I think you are going to find this is the same kind of town. We are the same kind of people." And the second man decided to drive on.

Another citizen of the town who had been sitting there with the storekeeper said, "Wait a minute! What do you mean by giving those two men two different viewpoints of this town?" And the storekeeper replied, "I've learned that any town will be the same kind of town that you have left—because you will be the same kind of person."

May I say to you, the child of God ought to recognize that he is not to be looking for someone to do something for him, but he is to be expressing love in real action and in real concern for others. "By this shall all men know that ye are my disciples, if ye have love one to another" (John 13:35). If you love the Lord Jesus, if you love your heavenly Father, you are going to love other believers. You will know that you are keeping His commandments, and they will not be a burden to you at all. The Lord Jesus said, "For my yoke is easy, and my burden is light" (Matt. 11:30). It will be heavy unless you have the real love for the Lord and you truly want to serve Him. Then church work and other ministries will never become difficult.

Dr. Ironside taught this epistle of John while I was in seminary, and he told us this story:

Some time ago I read of a man who spent a few months in India. When he came back, he was discussing India at the home of some of his friends, and the talk drifted to missions, and this man, out of his wide experience, about five months in India, said, "I have no use for missions and missionaries. I spent months there, and didn't see that they were doing anything; in fact, in all that time I never met a missionary. I think the church is wasting its money on missions." A quiet old gentleman sat near. He had not said anything, but now spoke up and said, "Pardon me; how long did you say you were in India?"

"Five months."

"What took you there?"

"I went out to hunt tigers."

"And did you see any tigers?"

"Scores of them."

"It is rather peculiar," said the old gentleman, "but I have spent thirty years in India, and in those years I never saw a tiger but I have seen hundreds of missionaries. You went to India to hunt tigers and you found them. I went to India to do missionary work and found many other missionaries."

It's owing to what you are looking for, my friend. Are you concerned about God's work today? Are you concerned about getting out God's Word? Some folk say, "Well, I don't see that much progress is being made." You just don't happen to be where the action is, for the Word of God is going out, and it is having its effect in hearts and lives.

For whatsoever is born of God overcometh the world: and this is the victory that overcometh the world, even our faith [1 John 5:4].

Since we hear so much about "victory" in the Christian life today, it may seem strange to you that it occurs so rarely in the New Testament.

What is it that overcomes the world? It is our faith. It is faith that saves us, and it is faith that keeps us. We are saved by faith; we walk by faith. We are born children of God by faith in Jesus Christ, and faith is the only way in which you and I will be able to overcome this world around us.

Now we have an enemy, and John has talked about this enemy before: "Love not the world, neither the things that are in the world (1 John 2:15). There is in the world that which is of the flesh, that which is of the world, and that which is of the Devil. As Wordsworth put it, "The world is too much with us." As believers we are in the world, but we are not to be of it. This world that you and I are in is a big, mean, bad world. We can be caught up in it very easily—we can be trapped by it.

There is an illustration of this in the Old Testament which I think might be helpful to us at this point. It is the story of Joshua and the children of Israel entering the Promised Land. First, I must say that the Promised Land is not a figure of heaven. Our songs which talk about Canaan being heaven and the place to which believers are going simply do not fit what God teaches us in His Word. Actually, Canaan represents a condition in which believers ought to be living down here. We can live out in the wilderness, and there are a great many wilderness believers today. They do not have any fun at all, although they think they do at times. There's no fun out in the wilderness. The wilderness march was not easy. But the land of Canaan is where we are blessed with all spiritual blessings.

When Joshua entered the land, it was not handed to him on a silver platter. If you and I today are to enjoy the spiritual blessings which are ours, we need to recognize that we have a battle to fight; the enemy holds the territory, and he is not going to let us have any kind of deliverance or victory without a battle. When Joshua entered the Promised Land, therefore, there were three enemies that stood before him. Until he overcame them, he was not able to take the land.

The first enemy was Jericho, and Jericho represents the world. That was the first place Joshua struck. It was obvious that what he was trying to do was to split the land into two divisions and then take one at a time. Then the second enemy was little Ai which represents the flesh. Joshua sent a small contingent up there, thinking it would be easy to take, but that is the one place where he received a telling defeat. Many Christians overcome the world, but they are always overcome by the flesh. In other words, there are many saints who don't engage in worldly practices, but they go to church and gossip—they indulge the flesh. They can blow the trumpet around Jericho, but they don't blow the trumpet around Ai. Then finally there were the Gibeonites who represent the Devil. They deceived Joshua. The Devil was a liar from the beginning. He still deceives and works wilily.

Let's come back to verse 4 and look at it in reference to Jericho. "For whatsoever is born of God overcometh the world." If you are a child of God, you are going to overcome the world. How will you gain the victory? "And this is the victory that overcometh the world, even our faith." It is not by fighting but by faith. How did this man Joshua overcome Jericho? Jericho was the enemy which was out in front of him, and he had to take the city. How was he going to take the city? By fighting it? He did not fight it at all, but God told him what to do. God said, "I don't want you to use a battering ram to try to get through the gate. The thing which I want you to do is to march around the city. Instead of putting only your elite army up in front—the Marines or the special guards—I want you to also put the priests up there with the ark of the covenant. And the priests shall carry horns, and the trumpets are to be blown as they go around the city. But you are not to make an attack upon the city." It was a most unusual method which God gave to Joshua!

I am confident that the city of Jericho had braced itself for the onslaught of these people who had crossed the Jordan River at flood stage—which must have seemed to Jericho to be an impossibility and a foreboding of things to come. So they shut up their city, ready to defend themselves against Israel. I think that their guard up on the gate gave the signal. "Here they come—the whole army of Israel!" As Israel marched up to the gate, you must remember that there was an army on the inside ready and waiting for them. But when the children of Israel came up to the gate, they made a right face and kept on marching. They marched once around the walls of the city, and then they went back into camp!

You can be sure that there was a meeting of the general's staff in the city of Jericho that night to try to figure out the strategy that Israel was using against them. As best they could, they prepared themselves for the next day when the guard on the gate again yelled down and said, "Here they come!" They braced themselves for the battle in case Israel tried to break through the gates. Probably there were soldiers up on top ready to pour boiling oil or water down upon them and to shoot arrows, but Israel didn't attempt to come through. They simply marched around the city again, and they repeated that for six days. By that time, the army staff inside the city of Jericho had just about gone crazy. They didn't know what in the world was taking place.

On the seventh day, when Israel had gone around one time, the general's staff heaved a sigh of relief and said, "It sure looks like they're not going to take that city. They are just doing something very crazy." From the world's viewpoint, it was very crazy—you must admit that this was an unusual strategy. But this time the guard said, "Wait a minute! They are not returning to camp. They are marching around again!" And Israel proceeded to march around the city *seven* times. Then what happened? The priests of Israel blew the trumpets, the people shouted, and the walls of Jericho fell down! The children of Israel probably completely encircled the city, and when the walls of Jericho fell down, the army on the inside was certainly taken by surprise.

How did the children of Israel take the city of Jericho? By fighting? They did not fight at all. They were marching around according to the order given not by Joshua but by that unseen Captain of the host of the Lord. Frankly, I used to have a problem with this incident in Scripture. My problem was not with the walls of Jericho falling down—that fact has been pretty well established by archaeological excavations—but the thing that disturbed me was why a man of Joshua's proven ability as a military leader would use tactics like this. It is true that God commanded it, but I still think that Joshua might have disagreed with the tactics.

The answer lies in that earlier incident when Joshua saw the man with the drawn sword standing at the edge of the Israelite camp (see Josh. 5:13–15). Joshua went out and said to the man—if you want it in good old Americana—"What's the big idea? Who told you to draw a sword?" Joshua's question was, ". . . Art thou for us, or for our adversaries?" (Josh. 5:13). That's the way our translation gives it, and it is a good translation, but probably Joshua really meant, "What's the big idea? Who gave you an order to draw a sword?" Joshua thought *he* was in charge. But when the man turned and answered, Joshua realized that He was a supernatural person. I personally believe that He was none other than the preincarnate Christ. Then Joshua fell at His feet and worshiped Him. So you see, before the battle of Jericho, this man Joshua learned that he was not really in charge. General Headquarters was not in his tent but in heaven with the Captain of the host of the Lord, for that is how the Stranger identified Himself, ". . . Nay; but as captain of the host of the LORD am I now come . . ." (Josh. 5:14). In other words, the Lord was telling Joshua, "This battle you are fighting is a spiritual battle as well as a physical one, and I'm the Captain." So General Joshua was now going to take his orders from the "captain of the host of the LORD," and the Captain said, "March around the city." With this incident in mind, I don't have any trouble understanding Joshua. If you had met him and asked him why in the world he was using such a crazy maneuver, I think he would have agreed with you, "Say, this is crazy, isn't it? But after all, I'm just taking orders."

If you have ever had any army experience, you know that a buck private never talks back to a captain. That is, when the captain says, "Go, do this," the private doesn't stop and say, "I've been thinking this over myself, and I think there is a better way of doing it." Did you ever hear of a buck private saying that to a captain? No! He says, "Yes, sir! I'll go do it." And he goes and does whatever the captain has commanded. When I was in the National Guard, some fellows got into trouble by slipping out during the night. The next day, the captain gave them an order to dig a hole. He said, "I want this hole six feet long, I want it three feet wide, and I want it five feet deep." The fellows dug the hole and then went in and reported to the captain. The captain came out, looked at the hole, and he said, "Now I want you to fill it back up with the dirt." They had to fill it back up! That sounds sort of crazy, but they had to obey orders.

Joshua was obeying orders. He was being obedient. He *believed* the Captain. Hebrews 11 tells us, "By faith the walls of Jericho fell down . . ." (Heb. 11:30). It wasn't by fighting or military skills but by faith that the walls of Jericho fell down.

What is the lesson for us today? You and I cannot overcome the world by fighting it. This is one reason that as a pastor I never engaged in any reform movement, no matter how worthwhile it was—and I agreed that many of them were good. I would never serve on the committee, nor would I have part in it as pastor of a church because I do not think I was called to get into that at all. You don't overcome the world by fighting it. I knew a former movie star many years ago who called me when I was a pastor in downtown Los Angeles and asked if I would serve on a committee to help reform downtown Los Angeles. Downtown Los Angeles needed reforming then, and it still does, but I never felt I was called to do that. I refused to serve on the committee, and she couldn't believe it. She said, "Do you mean to tell me that you won't serve on the committee? As a preacher you are not interested in that?" I said, "I didn't say that. I just won't serve on the committee." And I told her why. I said, "The Lord called me to fish in the fishpond, but He never told me to clean up the fishpond. So my business is fishing, giving out the Word of God. I let the Spirit of God do any cleaning up that's to be done. That is the department He is in, and I'm not in that department." She didn't like it, but she had to accept it, of course. I don't fight the world today. I'm not in any great reformation movement. I'm not trying to straighten up our government, although I think it needs straightening up. I think that both the Democratic and the Republican parties are in a shambles today. We are without leadership as a nation. Although I recognize all of this, it is not my business to try to change it. My business is to give out the Word of God.

Although he had the army, Joshua's business was not to fight. His business was to believe God. He believed God, and the walls fell down. My friend, today we are saved by faith, and if we are going to overcome this world, we'll not overcome it by fighting it. We are going to overcome it by faith. That is the only way you and I can deal with this world in which we live, and that is the great message which is here for us.

Who is he that overcometh the world, but he that believeth that Jesus is the Son of God? [1 John 5:5].

When you really trust Christ, it is not a question of your own power, but you are kept by the power of God through faith. We have faith in

Christ for salvation in the future and faith in Christ for salvation from the world here and now.

ASSURANCE OF SALVATION

This is he that came by water and blood, even Jesus Christ; not by water only, but by water and blood. And it is the Spirit that beareth witness, because the Spirit is truth [1 John 5:6].

You will recall that at the crucifixion of Jesus His bones were not broken in fulfillment of Scripture. In order to hasten death, the Romans would sometimes break the legs of those who were hanging on the crosses, but John tells us in his Gospel: "But when they came to Jesus, and saw that he was dead already, they brake not his legs: But one of the soldiers with a spear pierced his side, and forthwith came there out blood and water. And he that saw it bare record, and his record is true: and he knoweth that he saith true, that ye might believe" (John 19:33–35). John was present at the crucifixion of Christ, and he noted something that no one else noted. Chances are that he was closer to the cross than any of the other apostles. He noted that when that soldier pushed the spear into the side of Christ, there came out blood and water—not just one element, but both elements.

Here in his epistle John makes application of this. He emphasized it in his Gospel, and now he comes back to it here and says, "He that came by water." "Water" speaks of what? It speaks of the Word of God. The Lord Jesus said to Nicodemus, ". . . Verily, verily, I say unto thee, Except a man be born of water and of the Spirit, he cannot enter into the kingdom of God" (John 3:5). The water is the living Word applied by the Spirit of God. "He that came by water"—the Word of God that the Spirit of God uses. "And blood" refers to the death of Christ. "Even Jesus Christ; not by water only, but by water and blood."

"And it is the Spirit that beareth witness, because the Spirit is truth." It is the Spirit who can make these truths live. May I make this rather startling statement: The Lord Jesus told the disciples' that between His death and resurrection and the day of Pentecost they were to tarry in Jerusalem and to do nothing—they were not to witness. Why? They could not witness effectually without the Holy Spirit. Therefore, if anyone is to be saved, not only is Christ's redemptive death essential, but also that the Spirit of God work in hearts and lives. I am encouraged by letters from listeners to our Bible-teaching radio broadcasts because they demonstrate that the Word of God taken by the Spirit of God can apply the blood of Christ to hearts and lives. Christ died for our sins, but the Spirit of God must make that real to us. Only the Spirit of God can make the death of Christ real to you, and only the Spirit of God can make the resurrection of Christ real to you.

In verse 7 it looks as if there are added three more witnesses which are in heaven—

For there are three that bear record in heaven, the Father, the Word, and the Holy Ghost: and these three are one [1 John 5:7].

In a very scholarly presentation, Dr. A. T. Robertson states that this verse is not in the better manuscripts. I heard Dr. Robertson lecture when I was a student in seminary, and he probably knew more Greek than anybody who has lived in our generation. I remember that when he got up the first day to lecture on the Epistle to the Romans, he had a great big sheaf of notes. He didn't even look up at the class because he was busy just straightening out those notes. Then he looked up and said, "I don't see how the apostle Paul ever wrote the Epistle to the Romans without my notes!" Of course, everybody roared at that. Well, Dr. Robertson was a great Greek scholar, and he makes the statement that verse 7 is not in the better manuscripts but was probably written in the margin by some scribe. You must remember that the Bible at first was handwritten. The first book printed was the Bible, but that was not until Gutenberg invented the printing press which was a long time after John and his day. Evidently some scribe put what we have as verse 7 in the margin, and then later on another scribe came along and thought it was to be included in the text. There is nothing wrong with the verse, but we do need to recognize that it is not in the better manuscripts. If we want to be scholarly and accurate and to be able to defend the verbal, plenary inspiration of the Bible, we need to know these things.

In other words, there are not six witnesses presented here. The three in heaven given in verse 7 would do us very little good down here on earth, but it is the three witnesses on earth which we are concerned about and which have a direct bearing on us. That is what needs to be emphasized.

> **And there are three that bear witness in earth, the Spirit, and the water, and the blood: and these three agree in one [1 John 5:8].**

What is the agreement which these three witnesses have? Well, they agree in one purpose, that is, the purpose of presenting Jesus Christ as the Savior of the world who shed His blood upon Calvary and paid the penalty for our sins.

"There are three that bear witness in earth," and these three are right here right now. The Holy Spirit will take the Word of God and apply it to your heart. You are reading this book long after the time I actually wrote it. I believe that the Holy Spirit is here, leading right now as I write. When you read this, the Holy Spirit will be there to take His Word and apply it to your heart. He bears record, if you please, and He is a witness. His witness is that you might come to a saving knowledge of Jesus Christ.

How are you going to come to that knowledge? Through the Word of God. You see, the blood of Christ delivers us from the penalty of sin. The Word of God delivers us from the defilement of sin in the world today. This is my reason for being a fellow with a one-track mind. All I have ever emphasized in my ministry is the Word of God. I just have one tune that I play—I just have one message that I give. I hope it doesn't get too monotonous but, my friend, the Word of God is the only thing which can clean up your life even as a believer, and it is the only thing which will keep it clean. This is something very important to know.

We are living in a day when a great deal of attention is given to cleanliness, in fact, too much attention. You are led to believe that if you don't use a certain miracle bar of soap, you will be out of it, you may even lose your job, and certainly all of your friends are going to desert you. But if you use a certain brand—it's a "miracle" substance—it will clean you up, and even clean your clothes up. It will clean up everything but what is on the inside of you; it won't clean up that. Only the Word of God can do that.

The only true miracle cleansing agent in the world today is the Word of God. It can clean you up; it can save you: "Being born again, not of corruptible seed, but of incorruptible, by the word of God, which liveth and abideth for ever" (1 Pet. 1:23). For the Word of God presents Christ who shed His blood for your sins and my sins. He died for our sins; He was raised for our justification. Not only can it save you, but the Word of God can also keep you clean while you are down here. You can use every kind of spray deodorant there is, you can rub it on, you can pour it on, you can buy it in the giant economy size, put it in your swimming pool, and swim in it, my friend, but it won't clean you on the inside. Only the Word of God can keep you clean today. That is the thing which John is emphasizing here. These three bear witness on earth—the Spirit uses the water of the Word and applies the blood for our salvation. These three all agree in one—that is, they want to get you saved and keep you saved.

If we receive the witness of men, the witness of God is greater: for this is the witness of God which he hath testified of his Son [1 John 5:9].

I don't know about you, but many folk whom I have talked to have reached a credibility gap between themselves and the news media, the politicians, and all who are on television today. I'll be very candid with you that there are certain news commentators whom I won't listen to any longer. I know that they are doing nothing in the world but giving out propaganda. They are not giving facts. Everything they give is biased and distorted and twisted for a liberal position. Apparently, they are willing even to misinform you, and they are willing to withhold facts to gain their objective. I have come to the place where it does not matter who they are or to what party they belong. I have no confidence in politicians. Therefore, we are in a place today where it is difficult to receive the witness of men, but the interesting thing is that John Q. Public swallows it hook, line, and sinker. You can tell by the different polls which are taken that a man's influence or his popularity is determined by what the news media say about him. The biggest frauds in the world can be built up by the media—Hollywood, of course, has done this for years. Most people *do* receive the witness of men; they are taken in by it. If it is said over television or if it is put into print, they will believe it. There are many people who believe whatever they read or hear, but they will not receive the witness of God! Oh, my friend, the witness of God is *greater!*

"For this is the witness of God which he hath testified of his Son." God today is not giving out news on every subject. His news is good news, and it is about His son who died for us on the Cross. That is His message.

> **He that believeth on the Son of God hath the witness in himself: he that believeth not God hath made him a liar; because he believeth not the record that God gave of his Son [1 John 5:10].**

"He that believeth on the Son of God hath the witness in himself." If you have trusted Christ as your Savior, the Holy Spirit indwells you, and He testifies that these things are true. This is one of the great encouragements in teaching the Word of God by radio. Many people who listen have never seen me (I guess that may a good thing!), but they have the Holy Spirit indwelling them, and when they hear the Word of God, they accept it because the Spirit bears witness that they are hearing the Word of God. This is quite wonderful, and it is the greatest encouragement in preaching and teaching the Word of God, whether it be from the pulpit, over radio, or through the printed page.

"He that believeth not God hath made him a liar." When you don't believe God, you add to your other sins by implying that He is a liar. God says, "Trust Christ, and I'll save you." If you say, "I don't need Christ to be saved," then you are calling God a liar. I receive many letters like the one from a woman who thought that since she was a member of the church and did a lot of things, she was all right. She had to listen to the teaching of the Word of God for a long time before she realized that she was a sinner and that she needed Christ as her Savior.

"Because he believeth not the record that God gave of his Son." What is "the record"? John is going to tell us—

And this is the record, that God hath given to us eternal life, and this life is in his Son [1 John 5:11].

What is the record? "This is the record, that God hath given to us eternal life, and this life is in his Son." Eternal life is to have Christ. It boils down to this one point. This is the gospel in a nutshell. This is the simplest test that can be made—

He that hath the Son hath life; and he that hath not the Son of God hath not life [1 John 5:12].

"He that hath the Son hath life." He didn't say, "He that belongs to the church has life." You might say, "I'm a Baptist" or "I'm a Methodist" or "I'm a Presbyterian" or "I'm a Nazarene" or "I belong to the Church of God." It does not matter what church you belong to—your church membership does not mean you are saved. Then *what* does it mean to be saved? "He that hath the Son hath life." The question is: Do you have Christ? Is He your Savior? Are you trusting Him in such a way that no one on earth or in heaven can shake your confidence in Him? My friend, if you haven't come to that point, you haven't come anywhere at all. To be saved means you trust Christ, and it means you have Christ as your Savior. "He that hath the Son hath life." He's our lifeboat. He's our lifeline. He's our only hope. We are lost without Him, but if we have Him, we have life.

"And he that hath not the Son of God hath not life." My friend, can it be made any clearer than that? Let's forget about religion. Let's forget about all this churchianity. Let's forget about all this gimmickry that is going on today—taking little courses, going through little rituals, all that sort of thing. Forget about it, my friend! The important thing is: *Do you have Christ? Is He your Savior?*

This is the reason John has emphasized that Jesus is the Son of God. I want to say to you, He is wonderful. He is God manifest in the flesh. He is the only one who can save us. He is absolutely unique. There is no one else like Him. He's the only begotten Son of God. He died upon the Cross because He alone could pay the penalty for our sins. He rose again, and He is living right this moment at God's right hand for us. He is the living Christ. Do you have Him today as your Savior? That is the only question you need to answer. If you have Him, you have life—you are saved. That is the record. Do you believe God, or don't you believe God? If you don't believe Him, you make Him a liar.

My friend, John has this down right where you can get it. You cannot miss this. The only thing right now that will keep you from coming to Christ is the sin in your life that you don't want to give up. That is the only thing in the world which will stop you. That is the decision you make.

These things have I written unto you that believe on the name of the Son of God; that ye may know that ye have eternal life, and that ye may believe on the name of the Son of God [1 John 5:13].

John has a twofold purpose in writing this epistle: (1) "that ye may *believe* on the name of the Son of God"—that's salvation, and (2) "that ye may *know* that ye have eternal life"—if you have Christ, if you have believed Him, you have life. A great many people say, "I just want to believe that I have eternal life." The question is: Whom do you believe? Not *what* do you believe, but *whom* do you believe? Do you believe God? Do you believe the record that He gave? He says that if you have the Son, you have life. Now do you believe that? John didn't say if you feel like it or if you have joined something, but if you believe in the Lord Jesus Christ as your Savior. And if you have Him, then you have life.

This is the reason John has written this epistle—"that ye may know that ye have eternal life." This was also the purpose of the Gospel which John wrote: "And many other signs truly did Jesus in the presence of his disciples, which are not written in this book: But these are written [John didn't write everything, just certain things], that ye might believe that Jesus is the Christ, the Son of God [that's who He is]; and that believing ye might have life through his name" (John 20:30–31).

If you have the Son, you have life—John wants you to know that, and you honor God when you know it. That simply means that you are not making God a liar, but you're trusting Him. It is not a matter of how much faith you have or how you feel about it, it is whether or not you trust Christ. That's all important.

Having this assurance of eternal life will do something for our Christian life here and now—

And this is the confidence that we have in him, that, if we ask any thing according to his will, he heareth us [1 John 5:14].

Our assurance will give us confidence in prayer, and believe me, we need confidence in prayer. This word *confidence* actually means "boldness." "This is the *boldness* that we have in him." This assurance will give boldness in prayer to the child of God.

"If we ask any thing according to his will"—our prayer must be according to the will of God. If you and I are in fellowship with Him, walking with Him, then our prayer would be for God's will in every circumstance. George Müller put it like this: "Prayer is not overcoming God's reluctance. It is laying hold of His willingness." It is not trying to get God to do something which He is reluctant to do, but prayer is to be our thinking His thoughts after Him. This is the thing which gives us confidence when we turn to God in prayer.

"He heareth us." You can be sure that He not only hears our prayer, but He also answers our prayer. God will hear the prayers of His children, but He will not always answer them by giving us what we ask.

John is saying here that we can have the confidence that He will answer our request according to the way we pray—when we pray in His will.

> **And if we know that he hear us, whatsoever we ask, we know that we have the petitions that we desired of him [1 John 5:15].**

It is wonderful to know that you and I have a heavenly Father. If we are in fellowship with Him, if we are not regarding sin in our lives, and if there are no other hindrances to prayer in our lives, we are not going to pray selfishly. When we are walking in fellowship with Him, when we are following Him, we can have the confidence that He will hear what we ask and answer our prayer. We are not to come to Him with mistrust or in a begging attitude, but we are to come with boldness to ask that God's will be done.

> **If any man see his brother sin a sin which is not unto death, he shall ask, and he shall give him life for them that sin not unto death. There is a sin unto death: I do not say that he shall pray for it [1 John 5:16].**

"Death" refers here to *physical* death. It has no reference at all to spiritual death because the child of God has eternal life. John is saying that believers can commit a sin for which their heavenly Father will call them home; that is, He will remove them from this life physically, perhaps because they are disgracing Him.

Let us look at some people in Scripture who have committed a sin unto death. Moses and Aaron committed a sin unto death. You will recall that Moses got angry when the children of Israel kept begging for water and, instead of speaking to the rock as God commanded him, he smote the rock twice. He shouldn't even have touched that rock. It had already been smitten once before, and he should have rested upon that. The rock was to be an example and a type of Christ. Paul wrote, "And [the children of Israel] did all drink the same spiritual drink: for they drank of that spiritual Rock that followed them:

and that Rock was Christ" (1 Cor. 10:4). Christ died only once, and Moses spoiled the type by striking the rock twice. "And the LORD spake unto Moses and Aaron, Because ye believed me not, to sanctify me in the eyes of the children of Israel, therefore ye shall not bring this congregation into the land which I have given them" (Num. 20:12). There was for this man Moses a restoration in that he could continue leading. However, he began to plead with God to forgive him and to permit him to enter the land, but the Lord told him in effect, "Although I have restored you to your place of leadership, you are not going to enter the land." When Moses kept after the Lord, the Lord said to him, ". . . speak no more unto me of this matter" (Deut. 3:26). Moses and Aaron both had sinned a sin unto death—physical death.

In the New Testament we have another example of this in Ananias and Sapphira. They were a part of the early church, and they were guilty of a lie (see Acts 5:1–11). They had been willing to give a false impression to the early church; they were willing to live a lie. Because of that, God removed them from this earthly scene.

There is another incident of this mentioned in 1 Corinthians. Some of the people there had actually been getting drunk at the Lord's Supper, and they were missing the meaning of it altogether. Paul wrote to them, "For this cause many are weak and sickly among you, and *many sleep*" (1 Cor. 11:30, italics mine)—that is, they were dead. Paul is saying that they had committed a sin unto death.

Someone might ask at this point, "What is a sin unto death?" First, let me be clear that John was not speaking of an unpardonable sin. We are talking about a sin unto physical death, not spiritual death. These people were God's children. He would never have taken them home if they had not been His children. The Lord doesn't whip the Devil's children—He whips only His own. When His children sin unto death, He will take them home.

What is this sin? What is it specifically? Well, for Moses and Aaron it was one thing—they lost their tempers, and they destroyed a type of the Lord Jesus. Ananias and Sapphira were living like hypocrites. And in the city of Corinth, there were believers who were getting drunk and were disorderly at the Lord's Table. So a sin unto death is no one thing specifically. I have a notion that for you it would be different from what it would be for me, but I am of the opinion that every believer is capable of committing the sin unto death—whatever it is for him. You can go on in sin until God will remove you from the scene. This does not mean that every Christian who dies has committed the sin unto death, but it is possible to do that.

Absalom also committed a sin unto death. I believe that Absalom was really a child of God, but he led a rebellion against his father, King David. I have observed something over a period of years. I have watched how God has dealt with troublemakers in the church. I've not only seen Him remove them by death, but I've also seen Him set them aside so that they were of no more use in the service of God at all. It is possible to commit the sin unto death. Let me repeat that it is physical death not spiritual death.

Let me illustrate this. There is a mother who has a boy, Willie—her little angel child, of course. Next door, though, there lives a little brat about the age of her little angel, and they play together out in the backyard. One day as she is working in the kitchen, she hears that little brat yelling at the top of his voice. She rushes to the door, looks out, and there is her precious little angel on top of the little brat next door, just beating the stuffing out of him! She says, "Willie, you are going to have to come into the house if you are not nice to the little boy next door." He says, "Yes, Mama. I'll be better." She says, "Well, if you are not, I'm going to have to bring you in the house." So she goes back in, and about thirty minutes go by, but again she hears that familiar cry of the little brat next door. She goes to the door, and the same sight greets her. Her precious little angel is on top of the brat next door, just beating the stuffing out of him. She says, "Willie, come into the house." He says, "I don't want to come into the house." She says, "I said that if you did that again, you would have to come into the house!" So what does she do? She goes out and gets him by the hand, and she takes her precious little angel, yelling at the top of his voice, into the house. He had to come in. He may not be her precious little angel anymore, but he still is her son—that fact never was disturbed, but he can no longer play outside. I think that if a child of God goes on disgracing the Lord down here, the Lord will either set him aside or take him home by death. God doesn't mind doing that. I think He does it in many instances.

All unrighteousness is sin: and there is a sin not unto death [1 John 5:17].

Believers who are alive today have all sinned but we haven't sinned a sin unto death. We did something that was wrong, it was unrighteousness, but God didn't take us home. If He were taking home every believer who sinned, I would have been taken home a long time ago.

We know that whosoever is born of God sinneth not; but he that is begotten of God keepeth himself, and that wicked one toucheth him not [1 John 5:18].

"We know that whosoever is born of God sinneth not." As we have seen in this epistle, you and I have two natures: an old nature and a new nature. That new nature will not sin. It never sins but has a desire for God and for the things of God. That old nature *will* sin, and it is because of it that a believer does sin.

"But he that is begotten of God keepeth himself, and that wicked one toucheth him not." This is another verse which makes me believe that the child of God can never be demon possessed. I believe that Christians can get to the place where they are oppressed by demons, but if they are actually demon possessed, I would question their salvation—even though they may think that they are born again. Why? Because "greater is he that is in you, than he that is in the world" (1 John 4:4). The Holy Spirit would not be dwelling where a demon was.

And we know that we are of God, and the whole world lieth in wickedness [1 John 5:19].

This is the text of a sermon which I have preached on several occasions entitled "When the Devil Puts the Baby to Sleep." "And we know that we are of God, and the whole world lieth [actually, lies asleep] in wickedness [or, in the arms of the wicked one]." In other words, the Devil has the world asleep. The Devil is saying to Vernon McGee, "Sh-h-h. Hush! You're waking people up, and we don't want to do that! They are very comfortable. Many people in churches are dead in trespasses and sins, and we don't want to wake them up. Let's leave them alone." The Devil is concerned when people are awakened. You and I are living in a world that is asleep in the arms of the wicked one—if you look around today, you must agree with that statement.

And we know that the Son of God is come, and hath given us an understanding, that we may know him that is true, and we are in him that is true, even in his Son Jesus Christ. This is the true God, and eternal life [1 John 5:20].

My friend, Christianity is not a religion. It is a person, and that person is Christ. If you have Him, you have salvation—and it is not a religion.

John concludes his epistle by saying—

Little children, keep yourselves from idols. Amen [1 John 5:21].

Anything that stands between Christ and the believer is an idol. John says that you are to keep yourself from the things of the world which occupy your mind and your attention. Covetousness is idolatry; other things are idolatry. Many people are worshiping many things in this wicked world today. These things are nothing in the world but idols. God's first statement to us is: "In the beginning God created . . ." (Gen. 1:1). Among His last words to us are these: "Little children, keep yourselves from idols."

BIBLIOGRAPHY

(Recommended for Further Study)

Boice, James Montgomery. *The Epistles of John.* Grand Rapids, Michigan: Zondervan Publishing House, n.d.

Burdick, Donald W. *The Epistles of John.* Chicago, Illinois: Moody Press, 1970.

Ironside, H. A. *The Epistles of John.* Neptune, New Jersey: Loizeaux Brothers, 1931.

Kelly, William. *An Exposition of the Epistles of John.* Addison, Illinois: Bible Truth Publishers, 1905.

Mitchell, John G. *Fellowship: Three Letters From John.* Portland, Oregon: Multnomah Press, 1974.

Robertson, A. T. *Epochs in the Life of the Apostle John.* Grand Rapids, Michigan: Baker Book House, 1933.

Stott, J. R. W. *The Epistles of John.* Grand Rapids, Michigan: Wm. B. Eerdmans Publishing Co., 1964.

Strauss, Lehman. *The Epistles of John.* Neptune, New Jersey: Loizeaux Brothers, n.d.

Thomas, W. H. Griffith. *The Apostle John.* Grand Rapids, Michigan: Wm. B. Eerdmans Publishing Co., 1956.

Vaughan, Curtis. *1,2,3 John.* Grand Rapids, Michigan: Zondervan Publishing House, 1970.

Vine, W. E. *The Epistles of John.* Grand Rapids, Michigan: Zondervan Publishing House, n.d.

Wuest, Kenneth S. *In These Last Days.* Grand Rapids, Michigan: Wm. B. Eerdmans Publishing Co., 1954. (Deals with the epistles of 2 Peter, John, and Jude.)